THE WORKS OF SHAKESPEARE

EDITED FOR THE SYNDICS OF THE
CAMBRIDGE UNIVERSITY PRESS
BY
SIR ARTHUR QUILLER-COUCH
AND   JOHN DOVER WILSON

THE MERRY WIVES
OF WINDSOR

THE MERRY WIVES
OF WINDSOR

CAMBRIDGE

AT THE UNIVERSITY PRESS

1969

PUBLISHED BY

THE SYNDICS OF THE CAMBRIDGE UNIVERSITY PRESS

Bentley House, 200 Euston Road, London, N.W. 1
American Branch: 32 East 57th Street, New York 22, N.Y. 10022

Standard Book Number:

521   07546   7   clothbound

521   09489   5   paperback

First edition 1921

* *Reprinted* 1954   1964

First paperback edition 1969

* Places where additional changes or additions have
been introduced are marked wherever possible by a
date [1954] in brackets. See also p. 133 for additional Notes.

*First printed in Great Britain at the University Press, Cambridge
Reprinted in Great Britain by Hazell Watson & Viney Ltd,
Aylesbury, Bucks*

CONTENTS

THE MERRY WIVES
OF WINDSOR

I

Shakespeare wrote for the stage: and on the stage, in spite of many loose ends in the dialogue and (still worse) in the intrigue, *The Merry Wives of Windsor* seldom misses to please an audience[1] or to justify itself as one of the briskest, heartiest and most *playable* of comedies. It has had less luck in the library, the majority of its editors having taken it at once too seriously and not seriously enough: too seriously, being preoccupied with the text (one of the most tantalising in the whole canon) and with two famous legends which have attached themselves to the play; and not seriously enough, being prejudiced by one of these traditions—that *The Merry Wives* was a slight thing, turned off in a hurry to fulfil a royal command—and using this prejudice to explain their disappointment that its Falstaff does not satisfy their ideal conception of Falstaff derived from *King Henry IV*, Parts i and ii. For example Maurice Morgann, who in 1777 published a famous Essay *On the Dramatic Character of Sir John Falstaff*, simply ignored this play: which must mean that he found in it no significant portrayal of the man, or, at any rate, none congruent with the Falstaff of *King Henry IV*.

---

[1] We must except Samuel Pepys, who saw it, for the third time, on the 15th of August, 1667: 'Sir W. Pen and I to the Duke's house; where a new play. The King and Court there: the house full, and an act begun. And so we went to the King's, and there saw *The Merry Wives of Windsor*; which did not please me at all, in no part of it.'

We shall deal in due course with the legend which connects the opening lines of our play with a deer-stealing escapade for which Shakespeare in his youth had been (so the story runs) put to the law by Sir Thomas Lucy, Knight, of Charlecote near Stratford-on-Avon; its interest being personal and almost quite extraneous from our consideration of the play and its merits.

The other tradition—that Shakespeare wrote *The Merry Wives* under royal command and produced it in a fortnight or so—is obviously of far greater, indeed of capital, importance to the critic and the textual editor; and therefore we make it our starting-point.

II

We first pick up this tradition in 1702, in a dedicatory epistle prefixed by John Dennis to *The Comical Gallant*, an attempt to adapt and 'improve' *The Merry Wives*, of which he tells us:

First I knew very well that it had pleased one of the greatest queens that ever was in the world...This comedy was written at her command, and by her direction, and she was so eager to see it acted that she commanded it to be finished in fourteen days; and was afterwards, as tradition tells us, very well pleased at the representation.

In a prologue he repeats the story:

But *Shakespeare's* Play in fourteen days was writ,
And in that space to make all just and fit
Was an attempt surpassing human Wit.
Yet our great Shakespeare's matchless Muse was such,
None e'er in so small time perform'd so much;

and in his *Letters* he reduces the allowance to ten days.

In 1709 Rowe, in his *Life of Shakespeare*, expands the legend. Queen Elizabeth, he says,

was so well pleased with that admirable character of Falstaff in the Two Parts of Henry the Fourth, that she commanded him to continue it for one play more, and to show him in love. This is said to be the occasion of his writing The Merry Wives of Windsor. How well she was obeyed, the play itself is admirable proof.

A year later Gildon, in his *Remarks on the Plays of Shakespeare*, thus concludes upon *The Merry Wives*:

The Fairies, in the fifth Act, make a handsome compliment to the Queen in her Palace of Windsor, who had obliged Shakespear to write a Play of Sir John Falstaff in Love, and which, I am very well assured he performed in a Fortnight; a prodigious thing, when all is so well contriv'd, and carried on without the least confusion.

These are all the 'authorities' for the legend, which (as Malone conjectured) may have come down to Dennis through Dryden, who had it from D'Avenant. We must observe (1) that it crops up precisely a hundred years after our play first saw print, in a Quarto of 1602; (2) that Dennis was born in 1657, Gildon in 1665, Rowe in 1674; and (3) that the first-named allows Queen Elizabeth's delight in the play to be a 'tradition.' Indeed the whole story is that and no more.

Nevertheless we accept it. Apart from its *looking* true —apart from its signal advantage of relevancy over nine-tenths of the *Shakespeariana* commonly used to distend the biographies, and its merit of providing a lively hypothesis to account for certain definite difficulties in a particular play—we accept it with a confidence that grows experimentally as we apply the story and find it the key to other difficulties, to puzzles of which neither Dennis nor his informant could have been aware. Gildon, again, is right in opining that to compose [and produce?] *The Merry Wives* in a fortnight was 'a prodigious thing,' as he is wrong in adding that 'all is so well contriv'd, and carried on without the least confusion.' The plot, when analysed, almost resolves itself into confusion: yet the confusion can be accounted for—with the help of his anecdote.

III

But puzzles and problems so crowd themselves upon this play as to compel a preliminary word upon the texts in which it has come down to us[1]. For all practical purposes they are two: (1) the Folio of 1623, (2) a Quarto of 1602—so eminently a Bad Quarto that every editor finds himself inflexibly driven back upon the Folio version[2].

This looks like plain sailing. But, fortunately or unfortunately, the Bad Quarto can be cursed more easily than despised. Its history begins with a couple of entries in the Register of the Stationers' Company:

18 Januarij [1602]

Iohn Busby Entred for his copie vnder the hand of master Seton/A booke called An excellent and pleasant conceited commedie of Sir Iohn ffaulstof and the merry wyves of Windesor   vjd

Arthur Iohnson Entred for his Copye by assignement from Iohn Busbye, A booke Called an Excellent and pleasant conceyted Comedie of Sir Iohn ffaulstafe and the merye wyves of Windsor . . . vjd

In the same year Arthur Johnson [with Thomas Creede for printer] published his Quarto under the title:

A/Most pleasant and/excellent conceited Co-/medie, of Syr *Iohn Falstaffe,* and the/merrie Wiues of *Windsor.*/Entermixed with sundrie/variable and pleasing humors, of Syr

---

[1] A second Quarto appeared in 1619—a mere reprint of the first, with an altered title-page: a third Quarto in 1630, reproduced from the First Folio with some changes in spelling and punctuation. They need not concern us. Of the Folios, here as elsewhere, we use the First as the only one having authority.

[2] We discuss the provenance of the copy in detail on pp. 93–101.

Hugh/the Welch Knight[1], Iustice *Shallow*, and his/wise
Cousin M. *Slender*./With the swaggering vaine of Auncient
Pistoll, and Corporall *Nym*./By *William Shakespeare*./As
it hath bene divers times acted by the right Honorable/my
Lord Chamberlaines seruants. Both before her/Maiestie,
and else-where. / London / Printed by T. C. for Arthur
Iohnson, and are to be sold at / his shop in Powles Church-
Yard, at the signe of the/Flower de Leuse and the Crowne./
1602.

Every editor who tries to handle this Quarto has very
soon to admit that he cannot base a text on it. He may
hesitate among various ways of accounting for it (we
shall by-and-by suggest the likeliest), but its naughtiness,
as we have said, forces him back upon the twenty-years-
later Folio. And yet he must be constantly collating:
since, bad though it so obviously is, at any moment out
of the Quarto's chaos some chance line, phrase or word
may emerge to fill a gap or correct a misprint in the
better text. For an illustration or two:

(1) At 1. 1. 118, a gap in the Folio leaves us at a loss
concerning the ground of Slender's grievance against
Bardolph, Nym and Pistol. The Quarto supplies it con-
vincingly and deliciously—'They carried mee to the
Tauerne and made mee drunke, and afterward picked
my pocket.'

(2) At 3. 1. 99, a gap in the Folio deprives us of six
necessary words in the reconciling of Caius with Evans:

Giue me thy hand (Celestiall) so: Boyes of Art, I haue
deceiu'd you both.

The Quarto supplies

> Giue me thy hand terestiall,
> So giue me thy hand celestiall:
> So boyes of art I haue deceiued you both...

(3) For a last sample, at 4. 5. 94—the Folio makes
Falstaff say 'I neuer prosper'd, since I forswore my selfe

---

[1] A slip. The printer who set up the title-page had read
the play carelessly, no doubt.

at *Primero*: well, if my winde were but long enough; I would repent....' But the Quarto gives us

> and my winde
> Were but long enough *to say my prayers*,
> Ide repent...

with its addition inserting the true and only point.

For a single counter-illustration—to show how vicious the Quarto can be—a few lines before, when mine Host of the Garter learns that he has been robbed of his horses, it makes him cry out

> I am cosened *Hugh*, and coy *Bardolfe*

where the Folio teaches us to amend '*Hugh*, and coy' into 'Hue and cry!'

Now for our point.—As an editor goes on collating and comparing, the conviction is borne in upon him, not to be resisted, that these two texts, the bad and the better, cannot really be separated; that both must derive from some common original. It was Halliwell's theory that the Quarto gave a first rough draft of the play, the Folio a version vastly improved upon it. But this theory no longer holds water: since the labours of P. A. Daniel, and more recent critics[1] conclusively prove the Quarto to be no first sketch, but a compressed, 'cut down,' version of some pre-existent play, and the Folio a later, still imperfect, but far better version of the same.

IV

Having assured ourselves of this, we begin to examine our texts in the light of Dennis' tradition. They support it at once with evidence that the play was written in a hurry: and the farther we go into it the faster that evidence grows concurrently with evidence that the bulk of the play, as we have it, was written for a command performance before Queen Elizabeth, almost certainly

[1] For references see p. 101.

at Windsor itself[1], somewhere about the years 1598–1600.

We soon note, as we read, that while the main intrigue is worked deftly and runs intelligibly, the piece abounds with loose ends and threads that Shakespeare has failed to work into the texture: abortive plots, plots either addled or hatched out and designed to fly but dropped unfledged; with hints of other plots which at some time must have meant something but are left otiose. To take the opening scene—Justice Shallow has, it seems, come up from Gloucestershire to Windsor to lay complaint at Court against Sir John Falstaff for having poached his deer-park. He brings up with him, as witness, his cousin Master Abraham Slender, with further intent to fix up a match between him and the daughter of a comfortable burgher of Windsor, with a dowry. [As Parson Evans comments, 'Seven hundred pounds, and possibilities, is goot gifts.'] Master Slender has moreover a grievance of his own against Falstaff, whose henchmen—Bardolph, Nym and Pistol—have carried him into a tavern, made him drunk, and picked his pocket 'of seven groats in mill-sixpences, and two Edward shovel-boards, that cost me two shilling and two pence a-piece of Yed Miller.' Now here, for an opening, we have, out of *King Henry IV*, Part ii, one of the best-imagined foolish characters in Shakespeare, with a newly invented kinsman so true to blood and family feature that he positively enlarges the Cotswold estate in foolishness; the pair confronted with Falstaff in circumstances which promise a most admirable renewal and development of the old rivalry in mirth. But

[1] The fairies in Act 5 being enacted by Her Majesty's 'children of Windsor.' Several entries in Cunningham's *Accounts of the Revels at Court* (now vindicated for a genuine document) mention these 'children' with payments or rewards bestowed by the Queen for their performances. 'So that,' as Hart says, 'the materials for producing a Windsor play, children and all, were ready to her Majesty's hand.' On one occasion at least she summoned them up to London, to divert her.

what happens? Nothing, or next to nothing. Falstaff, that 'shouldering whale,' heaves the whole business off him in a sentence, and starts (in the third Scene) his real intrigue, in which Justice Shallow plays no part but that of a purely negligible spectator. At the end we look back and remind ourselves that this juicy character, who started so full of import and importance, really lost his wind in the middle of the very first Scene, and has been thereafter carried along perfunctorily until such time as he could be dropped unnoticed in a ditch [5. 2.].

So much for one loose thread. But our play contains another no less remarkable; in the imperfectly excised plot whereby our Host of the Garter [4. 5.] is robbed of his horses. Who contrives this plot, and why? Obviously Caius and Evans should be the conspirators, in revenge for the trick the Host has played over the *venue* of their duel; and as obviously Bardolph, the new tapster at the Garter, is the accomplice made to their hand[1]. As the texts run, they present us with a casual, almost meaningless, episode. For our part, we make no doubt that the play, at one time and in some form, included a scene of contrivance which, if we could recover it, would make the affair neat and intelligible.

At these two points then—points of construction and therefore of first importance—we find evidence of carelessness which we can only attribute to haste. Other signs which indicate haste are—

(1) The proportion of prose to verse, which is higher than in any other play of Shakespeare's. Indeed *The Merry Wives* is almost all prose[2].

---

[1] For Hart's view, which is somewhat different, v. note 4. 3. 1–2.

[2] We would not over-stress this as evidence of haste. Shakespeare has everywhere a most delicate sense of the separate capacities of verse and prose, and alternates them with an easy tact quite superior to rule. Nine-tenths of *The Merry Wives* naturally demands prose, and appropriately gets it.

(2) The vileness of the small amount of verse employed. It is, to be sure, so vile in general as to raise another question—Could Shakespeare, even in a hurry, have written it? Now we have admitted in our General Introduction that Shakespeare could, and often did, write extremely ill: and we there expressed our impatience with the critics who, finding a bad line in any play of his, seek to bastardise it upon some one of his contemporaries. But Shakespeare has a way of his own when writing carelessly or badly or even abominably: and we can catch no echo of the familiar poet, even at his worst, in these lines of Fenton's declaration of love to Anne Page:

Quarto, sc. 12, 11–15:
  Thy father thinks I loue thee for his wealth,
  Tho I must needs confesse at first that drew me,
  But since thy vertues wiped that trash away,
  I loue thee *Nan*, and so deare is it set,
  That whilst I liue, I nere shall thee forget.

Folio, 3. 4. 13–18:
  Albeit I will confesse, thy Fathers wealth
  Was the first motiue that I woo'd thee (*Anne:*)
  Yet wooing thee, I found thee of more valew
  Then stampes in Gold, or summes in sealed bagges:
  And 'tis the very riches of thy selfe
  That now I ayme at.

The author of the Quarto lines, at any rate, was neither Shakespeare nor any rival of Shakespeare's nor any poet at all: he was either a dishonest actor who could not deliver his stolen goods, or (as we believe and shall attempt to show) more probably the plotter of a wooden original on which, as on a mannequin, Shakespeare hastily draped his comedy.

(3) The play, as a piece of writing, starts with admirable vivacity; but lags, almost at midway, to tail off into careless or sorry stuff; and these slipshod passages multiply as we near the end—a characteristic of work done at a push against time

(4) On the other hand, we make less than some editors do of the 'confusion in the time-table'—especially in 3. 5.—as evidence of hurry. All we require of a comedy on the stage is an *illusion* of time—a sense that the events are happening in probable sequence at reasonable intervals. No doubt, if we set to work to enquire curiously and tick off the action by the clock, we invite trouble. We begin to tell ourselves that Master Page has married a good wife and is rewarded with plenteous and even protracted meals—as Milton would say, 'frequent and full'—but not (it would seem) with regular ones: that his feasts are moveable—nay, mercurial: that he invites you in heartily at any time, and you are always in time if you do not boggle over the course you begin upon—venison pasty, or pippins, or cheese—for the others will come around; and that his custom of early rising, carried to a virtuous excess, coincides in result with the opposite practice alleged of the Snark:

> Its habit of getting up late you'll agree
>   That it carries too far, when I say
> That it frequently breakfasts at five-o'clock tea,
>   And dines on the following day.

Yet if we persevere, remembering that the Elizabethans took breakfast (when they took it at all) at about 7 or 6 a.m., or even earlier, and dined at 11.30 or noon, we can construct a time-table plausible enough: as thus—

First Day:

1. 1.; 1. 2. Shortly before noon.

1. 3. Afternoon (after an interval long enough for Falstaff to return from Page's dinner to the Garter, and to write his love-letters).

1. 4. Afternoon. (Simple, dispatched in 1. 2., has just arrived at Dr Caius' as the scene opens.)

During the evening of this day, Falstaff's letters are received by the merry wives and Caius' letters by Evans and the Host, while the latter makes his arrangements for the duel.

Second Day:

2. 1. Early morning (before eight). Shallow's slip 'good even and twenty' (l. 177) may be a relic of an evening scene following 1. 4. in the earlier version; but 'You'll come to dinner, George?' (l. 141) shows it is morning and Shallow and Host are clearly on their way to the duel.

2. 2. About 8 a.m. (Pistol back at the Garter after his interview with Ford in 2. 1., 'Eleven o'clock the hour...better three hours too soon,' etc. (l. 285) makes 8 a.m. an appropriate time for this scene. *N.B.* 'Come to me soon at *night*,' ll. 246, 264; but Ford comes in the morning at 3. 5.

2. 3.; 3. 1. Between eight and ten. *N.B.* 'This raw rheumatic day' (3. 1. 44) suggests early morning.

3. 2. About 10.30 a.m. The clock strikes (l. 41) the half-hour, we suppose.

3. 3. About 10.30–11 a.m. At the end of the scene the dinner, to which Ford has invited Page, etc., is not quite ready (v. note 3. 3. 214).

3. 4. Shortly after noon. Page and his wife return from Ford's dinner in the middle of the scene (v. head-note 3. 4. and S.D. 3. 4. 67).

Quickly's 'another errand to Sir John Falstaff from my two mistresses' (l. 109) is an error: (i) there has been no opportunity for her to hear of this errand, (ii) 'what a beast am I to slack it' suggests that she hurries off to the Garter forthwith, whereas we find her in the next scene arriving in the morning. The words may have been actor's or stage-manager's gag, to work a bustling exit.

Third Day:

3. 5. About 8 a.m. Quickly gives Falstaff 'good-morrow,' tells him Ford goes 'this morning a-birding,' and bids him 'come to her between eight and nine.' Ford (Brook) later says ''Tis past eight already.'

4. 1. A little past 8 a.m. Quickly has called upon Mrs Page on her way from Falstaff's. William is setting forth to school.

4. 2. Between eight and nine. Ford has drawn Page, Shallow, etc. 'from their sport,' i.e. the 'birding.'

4. 3. Immediately after the previous scene—during the explanation of the wives.

4. 4. Following on 4. 2. (with an interval for the explanation).

4. 5.; 4. 6.; 5. 1. Also following on 4. 2. In 4. 5. Falstaff has just arrived at the Garter in Mistress Prat's gown, and Simple has followed him along the street. In 4. 6. note that Fenton has already had news of the Herne plot from Anne, possibly by Quickly's means.

Ford makes a slip at 5. 1. 12, where he should say 'this morning' instead of 'yesterday.'

The rest of the day is taken up with preparations by the various parties for the rendezvous at Herne's Oak.

5. 2.; 5. 3.; 5. 4.; 5. 5. The night of the third day. Note that Shallow (5. 2. 10) says 'It hath struck ten,' which is probably an error for 'twelve'; the rendezvous being ''twixt twelve and one' (4. 6. 19)[1].

(5) Lastly, to us a far more evident sign of haste is found in the futile, almost puerile attempts, here and there, to hitch this comedy of Elizabethan England back upon the days of King Henry IV—e.g. in Page's objection against Fenton (3. 2. 64) that 'the gentleman is of no having—he kept company with the wild Prince and Poins.' It becomes merely absurd when, towards the end of the Quarto, Falstaff is made to cry:

> What hunting at this time of night?
> Ile lay my life the mad Prince of *Wales*
> Is stealing his fathers Deare

[1] The above table reduces the time-errors in the Folio text to five: (1) Shallow's slip 'good *even* and twenty' at 2. 1. 177, when the time is early morning: (2) Falstaff's 'come to me soon at night' (2. 2. 246, 264), answered in 3. 5. by Ford's coming in the morning: (3) Quickly's 'another errand to Sir John Falstaff' (3. 4. 109), already explained: (4) Ford's slip 'yesterday' (5. 1. 12) for 'this morning': and (5) Shallow's 'ten' (5. 2. 10) ? for 'twelve.' Although all these five errors may be imputed to haste in the original planning, they might easily pass unnoticed on the stage, and certainly do not deserve the severe judgments of Daniel and others upon the time-sequence.

just after (in the Folio) the elf Cricket has been commanded to hie to Windsor and pinch the maids who have left the Castle hearths unswept, because

Our radiant Queen hates sluts and sluttery

—a line which, though spoken of the Fairy-Queen, might, with a bow to Elizabeth, be carried over as a compliment to Elizabeth herself.

V

But with this in mind—that the play is to all intents and purposes an Elizabethan one—almost entirely of that time, with its Cotswold games and its 'Sackerson' and its contemporary Windsor residents, their manners and customs, and its Herne's Oak at an age when Herne the Hunter really was a traditional ghost (*temp.* Henry IV 'neither born nor thought of')—we strike, in the Quarto, upon a single word, 'Garmombles' which, while in itself neither illuminating nor attractive by beauty of its own, is no less a clue than was the glimmer of daylight at the end of Sindbad's cave. The Folio version, when we arrive at the theft of mine Host's horses, indicates the culprits by making Parson Evans (4.5.67) break in upon the scene (at the heels of Bardolph) with

Haue a care of your entertainments: there is a friend of mine come to Towne, tels mee there is three Cozen-Iermans, that has cozend all the *Hosts* of *Readins*, of *Maidenhead*; of *Cole-brooke*, of horses and money...

In the Quarto Sir Hugh breaks in (after Bardolph and Dr Caius) with

Where is mine Host of the gartyr?
Now my Host, I would desire you looke you now,
To haue a care of your entertainments,
For there is three sorts of cosen garmombles,
Is cosen all the Host of Maidenhead & Readings...

Now in 1592—let us mark the date—a Count Müm-pellgart (in F. 'Duke *de Iaminie*,' in Q. transliterated to

'Garmombles'), who next year became Duke of Würtemberg, visited Queen Elizabeth at Reading and was received affably. He was at Reading from the 17th to the
19th of August; and went on to Windsor, where he abode
until the 21st, putting in some deer-shooting, visiting
Eton College, and carving his name on the leads of the
highest tower of Windsor[1]. In short, this German Count
made himself very much at ease in Sion, and seems to
have earned unpopularity by his pompous manners (he
rode with a retinue cased in black velvet) and more
especially by his trick of commandeering horses, under the
Queen's warrant, to take him from one town to another.
An entry, of Oxford, is significant. He was compelled to
remain in that city sorely against his will because no
post-horses could be procured. Now it may be that our
Cousin Mümpellgart had made himself something of a
nuisance and something of a figure of comedy with his
passion for post-horses free of charge; or again it may be
that in 1592 certain rogues played upon this notorious
itch by levying and stealing horses in his august name[2].
At any rate there was a scandal; and it lent itself to
laughter; and it happened in 1592.

But we have not done yet with Count Mümpellgart.
As Duke of Würtemberg he conceived a strong desire to
be Knight of the Garter; had a fixed idea that Elizabeth
had promised it to him; and annoyed her for some years

[1] A narrative of his visit to England, entitled *A Bathing
Excursion*, was written by his private secretary, Jacob
Rathger, and printed at Tübingen in 1602. This was
digested by Rye in *England as Seen by Foreigners*, 1865; and
the clue has been admirably worked by Hart in his Introduction to *The Merry Wives* (Arden Edn, 1904). See also
Daniel and Greg. Mümpellgart left our shores on Sept. 6th
after 'riding over from there with post-horses to visit
Rochester.'

[2] Cp. *Henry IV*, Part ii (5. 3. 142), 'Let us take any man's
horses: the laws of England are at our commandment.'

with reminders. At length in 1597—the date again
should be noted—she allowed his election, though the
insignia took a long while in travelling. They were at
length conferred upon him with pomp at Stuttgart on
September 6, 1603, by mission of James I.

Now here we have a topical allusion—and the further
we examine it the fuller we scent this play to be of
topical and personal allusions—which ('save Your
Majesty') was a neat side-hit of scandal in 1592 or 1593,
when the fun of Cousin Mümpellgart's visit was fresh
in men's laughter, or might anywhere in 1597–8, when
the Queen passed him for the Garter, be revived as a
back-hit at a command performance, a little audaciously,
but with some certainty of provoking a laugh or, at
least, a smile in the audience of courtiers. But the
business was stale in 1602, and allusion to it only
survives by accident in the word 'garmombles': and
King James comes to the throne, and our play is revived
for a court performance in 1604[1], by which time it
is staler yet. So out goes the last trace of 'cosen
garmombles' to make room for an indefinite 'Duke *de
Iaminie*' and a train of 'Cozen-Iermans': even as out
went the oaths that besprinkle the Quarto and no doubt
delighted Elizabeth (who was not squeamish) or, when
not excised, were watered down to pallor in the Folio
in fear of the new law against Blasphemy.

[1] 'By his Matis plaiers. The Sunday ffollowinge (Hallowmas Day) A Play of the Merry Wives of Winsor.'—*Revells
Booke.* The authenticity of this book of Accounts, long suspected for a forgery, has been well vindicated by Mr Ernest
Law (see our Introduction to *The Tempest*, p. xlv *n.*) and
is supported by Sir James Dobbie, Government Analyst,
upon analysis of the ink of the incriminated handwriting.
The question was re-opened while our *Tempest* volume was
passing through the press, and we had to speak with caution.
But in the upshot Mr Law's vindication has been handsomely
confirmed. We shall have more to say on this matter when
we come to *Measure for Measure.*

VI

We have brought together the salient difficulties of
the text, and so have reached a point at which we can
present our hypothesis to account for them and for the
process by which this play reached its form in the Folio
version—our hypothesis, that is, by partial adoption,
since Mr A. W. Pollard was largely responsible for
suggesting it[1]. We shall present it in the form of
a narrative, using positive words, because by so doing we
help future scholars to correct us where we are wrong:
but we ask the reader to bear in mind that we know
ourselves to be speaking hypothetically.

We believe, then, that *The Merry Wives* was produced in a hurry and in obedience to a royal command by
Elizabeth, who was just the sort of lady to order a
comedy of 'Falstaff in love.' But we do not believe for
a moment that Shakespeare and the Lord Chamberlain's
Players hatched out an entirely new play in a fortnight
—if only for the simple reason that this kind of thing
does not happen in real life.

What happened (we suggest) was this. The Company,
harried by this violent order, hunted out of their repertory a play, *The Jealous Comedy*, of which (be it admitted)
we know nothing save that they had performed it on
January 5, 1593; and turned Shakespeare upon it to work
it up. As part of its plot this comedy of 1592–3 contained
some topical fooling on Count Mümpellgart and a
'borrowing' of horses. On the face of it we think it
improbable that in January 1593 Shakespeare's company
had *two* 'jealous comedies' on the stocks.

But what kind of play was this *Jealous Comedy*, on
which we suppose Shakespeare busy as reviser? Well, it
was a play of *bourgeois* life, probably located in London,
with an intrigue based on some Italian tale.

We believe the original to have been a play of com-

[1] In *The Times Literary Supplement*, Aug. 7, 1919.

fortable middle-class life, because *The Merry Wives*, as we have it, is that in essence, and we cannot conceive of it as having been at any time, under any form, anything else. We believe that it dealt with London tradesmen and their wives; because certain passages in the Quarto cannot (by us at least) be accounted for otherwise. In the Quarto Dr Caius' closet is always a 'counting house.' What use should an eminent physician, practising at Windsor and in Court favour, have for this counting-house? Moreover, the house would seem to have had a stall outside it, since Caius bids his servant Rugby look out 'ore de stall' for the approach of Parson Evans in his fury. Also, and as Mr Hart has observed, the Quarto lines in the fairy scene—

> Where is *Pead*? Go you & see where Brokers sleep,
> And Foxe-eyed Seriants with their mase,
> Goe laie the Proctors in the street,
> And pinch the lowsie Seriants face...

'sound pure London.' We think it possible that this original play derived its plot from an Italian story, and maybe was taken from Tarleton's *Newes out of Purgatorie*, 1590. But in Tarleton's story (derived from Straparola and closely resembling *The Merry Wives* in plot) the lover is hidden in a tub, or 'driefatte' of feathers: whereas in a somewhat similar tale, *Il Pecorone* by Giovanni Fiorentino, he is pushed *sotto un monte di panni di bucato*, which directly suggests 'buck-basket.' And while in the Italian *novelle* the devices of women to spirit away their lovers are endless, we cannot help suspecting that 'buck-basket' was derived from some translation of *Il Pecorone* unknown to us. As Thoreau has observed, there *is* such a thing as circumstantial evidence, as when one finds a trout in the milk-jug. But—and we may as well announce it here once for all—we hold the quest after Shakespeare's 'sources' to be in general, and save when he is obviously working upon Holinshed or North's *Plutarch*, a sad and mistaken waste of labour.

Shakespeare did not sit down in a library and pick out books to hunt in them for his plots. He 'stole his brooms ready-made.' He worked upon old stage-material, as often as not, to refurbish it. No one can get at grips with the true problem of any text of his until he has bitten it deep in his understanding (1) that Shakespeare's plots were plots of the playhouse, derived from Heaven-knows-where, and (2) that his plays attained print in 1623 upon playhouse versions often after a considerable and (by us) incalculable amount of alteration with or without his authority.

VII

We take up our tale. It is possible that the original 'jealous comedy' of middle-class life had already undergone transformation into an Oldcastle play[1]—with the horse-stealing business included—before Shakespeare set to work on the 1598 revision. But far more certain (as Mr Pollard has shown) than any traces of Oldcastle are the tracks of the original philandering 'hero,' left uneffaced in Shakespeare's hurry: of a lackadaisical sentimental swain, Euphuistic in address. Now Falstaff, as we know, could parody that address to perfection ['As the camomile, the more it is trodden,' etc.]: but nothing can be farther than Euphuism from Falstaff's habitual speech, as nothing can be emptier of the true Falstaffian

[1] Dr Greg first raised this suspicion over Sc. 15 (l. 1305) of the Quarto—'Sir *John*, theres his Castle, his standing bed, his trundle bed,' etc.: and Mr J. M. Robertson, following this up, has shown that several of the Quarto verse lines in which Falstaff occurs lack a syllable which 'Oldcastle' would supply. See also our Note on 'bully-rook,' 1. 3. 3. But the whole Oldcastle-Falstaff imbroglio is an intricate question, to be discussed when we come to *K. Henry IV*, Pt i. We may observe here, however, that, although Shakespeare had to drop the actual name 'Oldcastle,' it persisted in public recollection, and he might have risked retaining some allusions to it, or even slipping in a few back-hits which his audience would understand and enjoy.

accent, than his answer to Ford (2. 2. 221), 'Would it
apply well to the vehemency of your affection, that I
should win what you would enjoy? Methinks you prescribe
to yourself very preposterously'—unless it be his sancti-
monious words of repentance (5. 5. 117):

And these are not fairies! I was three or four times in
the thought they were not fairies—and yet the guiltiness of
my mind, the sudden surprise of my powers, drove the
grossness of the foppery into a received belief, in despite
of the teeth of all rhyme and reason, that they were fairies.

These and some few other utterances of his—besides
a tendency on the part of Mistress Quickly and others
to impute scholarship to him, of all virtues!—convince
us that the gross bulk of Falstaff was superimposed
upon an attenuated prig of a character, whose wrigglings
Shakespeare just misses, through haste, to stifle.

Shakespeare in his first scene opens with verve upon
the true Falstaff, and most admirably. But his hand
tires; his flats are not joined; and as the play proceeds
he (or somebody) inclines more and more to scamp the
job of adaptation. And the Queen might command, but
art and nature alike forbade him, to represent Falstaff,
cuddler of Doll Tearsheet, as 'in love' in any sense under
which that term can be extended to cover Romeo or
Othello, or even Biron or Orlando or Benedick. The
command suits well with what we know of Elizabeth;
and, if it be not blasphemy to question Shakespeare's
performance, he might have obeyed it more artistically
by presenting Sir John to us as *infatuated*—there being
proverbially no fool like an old fool. Instead, and in his
hurry, he chose to catch at this plot and present him to
us as a deliberate and mercenary intriguer, immoral even
beyond the stomaching of his retainers, Pistol and Nym:

There is no remedy: I must cony-catch, I must shift...
Briefly: I do mean to make love to Ford's wife...I have
writ me here a letter to her: and here another to Page's

wife...I will be cheaters to them both, and they shall be exchequers to me...We will thrive, lads, we will thrive.

Here, in brief, is the mainspring of the action: but it retorts Italianate intrigue upon the genial English opening, and so as almost to kill it. The plot, definite to hardness in patches—that Italian hardness which gives a story by Boccaccio the precision of a police-report—in places flounders in a mizmaze of quags, and almost founders. But the vitality of the characters, the vivid pictures of Windsor and of Windsor life, redeem the plot; while, to pull it through, there is ever the resource of Shakespeare's hand which, however tired, never lost its tact of the theatre. In the end he has done his task and fulfilled the royal behest with a thoroughly actable play, stuffed full with topical allusions for Her Majesty's mirth.

VIII

At this point comes in the rogue who reported, or dictated, large portions of the Quarto version. He was (as Dr Greg sufficiently proves) an actor who took at some time the part of mine Host of the Garter: for not only are mine Host's speeches far more accurately given than those of any other player, but the scenes in which he appears are always rendered more accurately than those which omit him; and, to quote Dr Greg, 'when he disappears for good and all, at the end of the fourth act (and the actor very likely went home or to the tavern), we find what remains of the play in a more miserably garbled condition than any previous portion.'

To sum up: we hold it demonstrable (a) that the Folio text derives from a play written by Shakespeare (with help, perhaps, from others), under royal command, in 1598 or thereabouts; (b) that this play was improvised (almost) upon a pre-existent 'jealous comedy' of middle-class London life, of date about 1593 and having a high-falutin Euphuistic lover for its victim; (c) that Shakespeare worked the transformation, but that his hand tired; and (*d*) that the Quarto gives a version of this feat of Shakespeare's conveyed to the printer by a rascal actor, who possessed some kind of text of the earlier 'jealous comedy' to fall back upon when his memory gave out.

IX

We emerge from this thicket of difficulties with a sigh of relief which, we have no doubt, will be echoed in double by the reader. But we emerge, at any rate, upon one of the pleasantest brick-and-green open spots in Elizabethan England; upon Windsor by the Thames, with its royal castle crowning the slope high over the river, and, around it and beside, a comfortable well-kept town, all the inhabitants whereof dwell within easy stretch of green fields, stiles, and such simple sports as that on which intent Izaak Walton would start, a few years later, from the City of London, up Tottenham hill, to fish the River Lea for chub and bring back 'the herb called heart's ease.'

Upon this setting, and among these honest provincial burghers, Falstaff and his rogues intrude with a very pretty contrast and promise of comedy to come; as they proceed to play it very happily and with no more infraction of the probable than may be allowed to a comedy impinging upon farce. It is rubbish to say that the Falstaff who played confederate in the Gadshill business and 'receiver' at least in the affairs of Master Shallow's venison and Mistress Bridget's fan, was incapable of amorous double-dealing with Mistress Page and Mistress Ford as a means of gilding his pockets and refurbishing his ragged and clamorous retinue.

What then is the matter? Well, the mischief, we hold, lies partly in us and our preconceptions: and we think this may be put most obviously in the matter of Mistress Quickly. She is sib to the Mistress Quickly whom we left in London, in charge of the beadles, and shall meet

in London again (*Henry V*), married to Ancient Pistol
and somehow restored to her old disorderly charge of
the Boar's Head, Eastcheap. We may, if we choose, tell
ourselves that she is far too nearly sib to be accounted
for as a sister-in-law; and, if we choose (and in defiance of
history[1]), invent a theory of a Mistress Quickly purging,
or having purged, her offence, and taking a temporary
rest-cure as housekeeper or 'in the manner of his nurse,
or his dry nurse, or his cook, or his laundry, his washer
and his wringer' to Dr Caius, French physician at
Windsor. But the question is, If Shakespeare had chosen
to call her Mistress Chickley—as he chose to substitute
a Slender for a Silence—should we not all be praising
this woman of *The Merry Wives*, with her hopeless (but
unjudged) morality, her rambling head, her sinful ir-
relevancies and indelicacies of tongue and conduct, as one
of the best of Shakespeare's minor inventions in Comedy;
ranking her, for example, at least as high as Dogberry[2],
and maybe tempted to set her above her original in
King Henry IV?

In fact when we carp at the Quickly of *The Merry
Wives* we are paying tribute to Shakespeare's unrivalled
power of transforming any given 'character' into a real
person. We take these folk to intimacy, to affection: we
follow them from play to play as in real life we follow
the adventures of a friend; and if, in any separate play,
the author's whim makes any one of them behave otherwise than we suppose ourselves to have a right to expect,
we feel that a tried friend has betrayed our trust: and in

---

[1] For, of course, 'the mad Prince of Wales' had left off
stealing his father's deer and was crowned King before
handing Mistress Quickly to the beadles. Moreover, at their
first meeting in this play, Falstaff does not recognise her.

[2] Whoso would permeate his mind with the essential oil
of Shakespeare's comic humour is advised to study the
Dogberry Scenes in *Much Ado about Nothing* and the Latin
Grammar Lesson (4. 1., purely episodic) in our play.

friendship this is not, however trifling, a matter of degree only. 'We had never looked for this in So-and-so. It may not seem to matter; the lapse is not so deep as a well, nor so wide as a church door, but 'tis enough, 'twill serve, we had given our confidence to him, and it turns out that the man was hiding this small secret all the while.' The rose, *under its own name*, no longer smells as sweet.

We might apply this parable of Mistress Quickly to Falstaff and put it bluntly, asking, 'Since a play is a play, and not a series, what right have we to drag in a prejudice from other plays? Take *The Merry Wives* by itself: dismiss from your mind this traditional command by Elizabeth: suppose that Shakespeare had chosen to call his hero Sir Toby Belch or Sir Anything Else instead of Falstaff; and then say, What grudge is left to you?'

The question might not be easy to answer: but it is answerable, and moreover indictable as not quite honest. For the Falstaff of *The Merry Wives* is the Falstaff of *King Henry IV*; his wit functions in the familiar way and his speech has all the wonted accent. Witness his discourse with Pistol in 2. 2.:

Falstaff. I will not lend thee a penny.
Pistol. Why, then the world's mine oyster,
Which I with sword will open.
Falstaff. Not a penny: I have been content, sir, you should lay my countenance to pawn: I have grated upon my good friends for three reprieves for you and your coach-fellow, Nym; or else you had looked through the grate, like a geminy of baboons: I am damned in hell for swearing to gentlemen my friends, you were good soldiers and tall fellows...and when Mistress Bridget lost the handle of her fan, I took't upon mine honour thou hadst it not.
Pistol. Didst thou not share? hadst thou not fifteen pence?
Falstaff. Reason, you rogue, reason: think'st thou I'll endanger my soul gratis?...

With what unction, in that last sentence, the great dewlap rolls up its gutturals, chuckling through deep envelopes, integument after integument of flesh! No: the Falstaff of *The Merry Wives* is the genuine man—the 'unimitated, unimitable Falstaff,' *totus teres atque rotundus*—bating some scattered twenty lines or so that were never written for him but belonged to the Joseph Surface amorist of the original. The excision of these (if we had the pluck, as editors, to make it) would remove the fly from the ointment; would allay the irritation which the presence of a 'foreign body,' however minute, sets working in the critical mind as in the physical system. Such particles—relics, as we contend, of the original amorist—as Falstaff's 'Would it apply well to the vehemency of your affection,' etc. which we cited just now, are grit in the critical eye, drawing tears out of proportion to their size. But they stick in the text, alas! and we must faithfully include the nuisances.

X

Of Falstaff's retainers, Bardolph is Bardolph to the end of his bulbous red nose. (One is sorry for his taking-off, in *Henry V*. His thefts, as his master warns him, are 'too open.') By nature he is the honestest of the gang, as he is the first to be provided for: and we think it significant that Falstaff gets him out of the way before broaching to Pistol and Nym a design against which even those warriors find a kick left in what remains of their conscience. The origin of Pistol has not yet been discovered, though we make no doubt that it must be looked for—as some day, perhaps, it will be found—among the old 'bombast plays' of the period: since, to our surmise, he is either a travesty or nothing[1]. At any rate here he

---

[1] Steevens, commenting on the line (1. 3. 20)

> O base Hungarian wight: wilt thou the spigot wield?

(in Q. 'Gongarian'), says that he remembers reading in 'one of the old bombast plays' the line

> O base Gongarian, wilt thou the distaff wield?

which unfortunately he 'forgot to note.'

reappears from *King Henry IV* with not one hackle of his plumage abated. As for Nym and his 'humours' —well, we shall hazard a guess about Nym, with the caution that it be taken for a guess and no more. He is, even more plainly than Pistol, a character of travesty, and the humour of his 'humours'—which, to tell the truth, lacks sap for us in our ignorance of the occasion— would as obviously become more juicy for us if more intelligible; if we but knew just what, or whom, it is travestying. We invite, then, the reader's consideration of the following facts:

(i) Between 1599 and 1602 there raged a wordy stage-war between the 'University wits' and the theatre-men; it started upon Jonson's quarrel with Dekker and Marston: it spread: and, as everyone knows, each party publicly lampooned its opponents, dragging them on to the boards under the thinnest of disguises and not sparing even their personal deformities of face, gait or gesture.

(ii) Though Shakespeare was evidently the champion figure among the theatre-men, we find no direct evidence in his plays that he struck a blow in this quarrel: and yet we have it plainly written in the University play —acted in St John's College, Cambridge, in 1601—

Why here's our fellow Shakespeare puts them all down, ay, and Ben Jonson, too. O, that Ben Jonson is a pestilent fellow. He brought up Horace, giving the poets a pill; but our fellow Shakespeare hath given him a purge that made him bewray his credit.

The words are put into the mouth of Kemp the actor, and Burbage his fellow-actor is made to answer 'It's a shrewd fellow indeed.' Now no commentator has been able to discover when, where, or in what form Shakespeare administered this alleged 'purge.'

(iii) The controversy, on its literary side, hinged itself upon Jonson's classical theory of the Comedy of Humours. He exemplified this theory in *Every Man in his Humour*, in 1598—the likeliest date of *The Merry Wives* and the most promising for a prompt counter-blow: he followed it up, next year, with *Every Man out of his Humour*; and Corporal Nym with his 'humours' reappears in *King Henry V* to cap it. There is no Nym in either part of *King Henry IV*. 'Humour' was the cant term of the whole dispute, and remains so in any historical discussion of it.

(iv) Jonson had seen military service in the Netherlands, and was entitled to boast (or, anyhow, did boast) that he had killed his man there and taken the '*spolia opima* from him': so that his stage-promotion to 'Corporal' would be taken up instantly by the audience.

(v) Jonson notoriously suffered from physical (as well as other) swellings of the head. Cf. Nym (1. 3. 88): 'I have *operations* [in my head] which be humours of revenge.'

(vi) Finally, the tradition is firm that, about this time, Jonson was starring the provinces as Hieronimo, Marshal of Spain, in Kyd's *Spanish Tragedie*. Now the 'short' for Hieronimo or Hieronymo is 'Nym,' with a side-glance at 'nim'=to steal.

Putting these facts together, we suggest that here may lie the explanation of that mysterious 'purge' which Shakespeare at one time gave to the great Ben, introducing him into this topical and rather scandalous play as Corporal Nym, prating of his 'humours,' reiterating the word until its boredom becomes comic, under a make-up which ridiculed Jonson in person and even in face. We drop this suggestion, and run for our lives.

No one can doubt, at any rate, that the part of mine Host of the Garter ridicules some actual personage; possibly the very landlord who in those days kept the famous hostelry. He is too individual—eccentrically, and, for dramatic purposes, purposelessly individual—to lie within the compass even of Shakespeare's invention: or (lest that assertion imply a presumptuous attempt to set bounds to his almost limitless range) let us put it rather that to any audience not 'in the know' and unable to refer the skit to some one in particular, this extravagant personage must have been a most improbable possibility. To *our* ears, at any rate—while we can accept Pistol for a type, and Pistol's lingo as a parody of something *generic*, and Nym, if we please, for a *sort* of idiot (the bore, familiar to us all, who thinks it funny somehow to reiterate a catchword)—mine Host has a habit of speech so peculiar as to indict him for a *particular* caricature. Caius may be another: but Caius in this play which Shakespeare overcharged—for the Queen's merriment, no doubt—with eccentric characters, is even more of a mystery than the Host. We can make nothing of the attempts to identify him with Dr John Caius, re-founder of a very famous house of learning now known as Gonville and Caius College, Cambridge. That eminent physician and anatomist (1510–1573) was an Englishman born and bred—'Caius' being but a Latinised form of 'Keys' or 'Kees'—and there is nothing to connect him with the French doctor in our play save (if it be remarkable of that age) an antipathy to Welshmen suggested in one of the College Statutes and long since corrected[1]. But he had been the most renowned physician of his time, and court attendant upon three sovereigns, Edward VI, Mary, and Elizabeth herself. So here comes in the puzzle, which we can only state and leave, with no pretence at being able to solve it[2]. The 'French Doctor' may have been a fashionable butt on the boards: he reappears in *The Return from Parnassus*; and Steevens cites, from Jack of Dover's *Quest of Inquirie* (1604), a tale entitled 'The Foole of Winsor' and beginning: 'Upon a time, there was in Winsor (quoth another of the jurie) a certaine simple outlandish doctor of phisicke, belonging to the Deane, who on a day being at Eton College....'

[1] Statute XII: 'Nullum praeterea deformem, mutum, caecum, claudum, mancum, mutilum, *Wallicum*...eligendum vobis esse: et si eligatur, excludendum constituimus.'

[2] But v. note 1. 2. 1.

But how did Shakespeare dare to employ, in the Queen's own presence, the name of 'Caius' for his invented figure of fun? We can only suggest that there was a French quack-doctor at Windsor in 1598: and that Shakespeare, caricaturing him 'to the life,' by a most audacious stroke of metonymy called him by the name of that revered predecessor whom he least resembled.

Evans is a delight from start to finish: but, as we have said, the play is overcharged with eccentrics, whose abuse of 'God's patience and the King's English' would be wearisome were it not so admirably qualified by its setting in normal England and the core-deep health of custom and conduct in its local habitants. Ford has a bee of jealousy in his bonnet; but suspicion of cuckoldry is an instrument which, from the beginning of time, Comedy has claimed to herself for a licensed gadfly to sting the comfortable. Shakespeare learned later to explore its tragic possibilities terribly, fatally: but in this play he confines himself to the conventional fun of it as Labiche (let us say) presents it in *Célimare le Bien-Aimé* or *Le Plus Heureux des Trois*. Ford at bottom is obviously a good fellow: Page, even more obviously, a mighty good fellow: and their two wives (to fall in with the play's own sporting habit of speech) as sound as bells and clean as two whistles. They show as honest, the pair of them, as they are 'merry,' and leave us to reflect at the conclusion that Master Page and Master Ford were a pair of lucky men; not the less lucky for having wives whose virtue contained a kick of mischief.

Further to make fragrant our jollity—with such fragrance as hawthorn wafts upon the fresh gale of Spring— we have sweet Anne Page, 'which is daughter to Master Thomas Page, which is pretty virginity,' and as genuinely English as the child that set *Venator* musing, 'I now see it was not without cause that our good Queen Elizabeth did so often wish herself a milkmaid all the month of May.' Shakespeare, never so happily sure of himself as in portraiture of a husband-high maiden, never drew one with more economy of touch. She says very little, but everything she says helps an outline so charmingly real that at the close of the first scene when she finally persuades Slender to walk before her into the house, we editors had written (but afterwards in cowardice erased) a stage-direction '*He goes in; she follows with her apron spread, as if driving a goose.*' 'As honest a maid as ever broke bread,' protests Quickly; 'but indeed she is given too much to allicholy and musing': which indeed again came naturally to a maid of Anne's age in Shakespeare's time, however her successors (who, after all, had mothers) may nowadays have trained their ambitions to repress or overshoot the primal instinct which populates human society and recreates the race.

> When as the rye reached to the chin,
> And chop-cherry, chop-cherry ripe within,
> Strawberries swimming in the cream,
> And schoolboys playing in the stream;
> Then O, then O, then O, my true love said,
> 'Til that time come agen
> She could not live a maid!

And truly Slender is a goose, and a goose to say grace over. His elder kinsman Shallow starts well but fades out, the action providing him with no nerve of motive. We re-greet him for old sake's sake; but we attend to him mainly because of his coat-of-arms and its 'dozen white louses,' and the implicated gibe upon Sir Thomas Lucy of Charlecote, Knight.

We must deal with the story here: but we shall deal with it as succinctly as we may, because it has actually little to do with our Comedy; it concerns the biographer rather than the critic or textual editor, and we have no intention of adding a Life of Shakespeare to our labours. Rowe starts the tradition (in 1709) of the old trouble between Shakespeare and Sir Thomas Lucy, who owned a coat of arms containing the heraldic luces, and of an old grudge repaid. Here is the passage:

He [Shakespeare] had by a misfortune common enough to young fellows, fallen into ill company; and, amongst them, some, that made a frequent practice of deer-stealing, engaged him with them more than once in robbing a park that belonged to Sir Thomas Lucy of Charlecote, near Stratford. For this he was prosecuted by that gentleman, as he thought, somewhat too severely; and in order to revenge that ill-usage, he made a ballad upon him, and though this, probably the first essay of his poetry, be lost, yet it is said to have been so very bitter that it redoubled the prosecution against him to that degree that he was obliged to leave his business and family in Warwickshire for some time and shelter himself in London.

Archdeacon Richard Davies, of Gloucestershire, confirms this at the end of the seventeenth century (and, it would seem, independently), with hearsay that Shakespeare was

much given to all unluckiness in stealing venison and rabbits, particularly from Sir Thomas Lucy, who had him oft whipt, and sometimes imprisoned, and at last made him fly his native county to his great advancement.

Almost everyone agrees that the story has a substratum of fact, and that in the first scene of our play, years afterwards, Shakespeare took his little revenge: and what a careless, good-humoured revenge it is, after all!—a line or two by a dramatist, rising to eminence in London, upon a local grandee who had, once on a time, dealt with him, a tradesman's son, given to wildness, with severity for his good. Too much of vindictiveness has been alleged upon a very innocent passage. Country-bred Englishmen habitually laugh at one another, and at their social 'betters,' without a trace of malice. If a foreigner interferes, Heaven help him! But we are neighbours and understand one another's little ways. Stratford-on-Avon is the centre of our world, after all; and we go back to it proudly, with a coat of arms of our own, and buy land, and die respected.

We think that Hart's comment sums up the matter in words on which it would be hard to improve:

> If we had no tradition, what should we make of the coat of arms passage? It would be utterly unmeaning. On the other hand, if we had not that passage, I doubt if any one so inclined could be prevented from rejecting the whole tradition.

But we have the passage: and where is the harm, either to Lucy or to Shakespeare, in accepting the tradition? Incidentally our acceptance of it helps the date we have already guessed for *The Merry Wives*. For Sir Thomas Lucy (a man notable, in his time, beyond the confines of Warwickshire) was dead in 1600: and it is conceded that Shakespeare was not the man to make a mock of him soon after his decease.

Still our interest in this famous passage remains an antiquarian one and should not be comparable, for liveliness, with our interest in the allusions to Cotswold life and sport that teem throughout this play, in which Shakespeare gets back from London to the country, if not so far as to his native midland, and lies and kicks his heels in joy of old liberty recovered. For Cousin Slender has come up to Windsor, a fool who is meat and drink; cousin Abraham Slender with his cane-coloured beard, and a-wooing too. Slender shall be explored and carved 'as a dish fit for the gods': Slender ever hovering on the verge of nonentity; at a loss how to woo without first aid from his small but scattered library:

> 'I had rather than forty shillings I had my Book of Songs and Sonnets here...How now Simple, where have you been? I must wait on myself, must I? You have not the Book of Riddles about you, have you?'
> 'Book of Riddles? why, did you not lend it to Alice Shortcake upon Allhallowmas last, a fortnight afore Michaelmas?'

It is, says Hazlitt, 'a very potent piece of imbecility...the only first-rate character in the play, but it is in that class. Shakespeare is the only writer who was as great in describing weakness as strength.' And his valour!—'I have seen Sackerson loose.' As Hartley Coleridge noted, Othello could not brag more amorously.

XI

The fairy scene at the close—borrowed perhaps from Lyly's *Endimion*, wherein the elves sing as they pinch Corsites black and blue—is pure harlequinade or extravaganza, but happy enough as the ending of a piece of foolery presented at Court: and the stage-directions which, in Quarto and Folio alike, assign the part of the Fairy-Queen to Quickly and make her utter lines so dissonant from her habitual chatter, as—

> And nightly, meadow-fairies, look you sing,
> Like to the Garter's compass, in a ring,

or

> Corrupt, corrupt, and tainted in desire!

merely mean that the boy who played Quickly made a 'lightning change' and shaped himself to this part also. The whole business, in short, is a romp, after curds and cream, courtship, bird-fowling and 'Frogmore over the stile.'

We make no apologies to the reader for the length of our introduction to this most teasing comedy. We suspect that the play provoked some scandal when it was first produced. We fear that it still, by obstacles we have tried to remove, scandalises the ordinary reader so that it has never yet been rated at its true merit. For ourselves we can only say that the longer we have puzzled over it, the more a sense of its jollity has grown on us; that, more almost than any other, it makes us feel what Ben Jonson had in wistfulness when he wrote:

> Sweet Swan of Avon! what a sight it were
> To see Thee in our waters yet appeare,
> And make those flights upon the bankes of *Thames*
> That did so take *Eliza* and our *James!*

1921   Q.

P.S. [1954]. A good deal of work has been done on this play since 1921 so that the foregoing introduction is of necessity out of date to some extent. Readers may be referred to the following:

E. K. Chambers, *William Shakespeare*, 1930, vol. i, ch. ix, § xxiii.

Leslie Hotson, *Shakespeare versus Shallow*, 1931.

J. Crofts, *Shakespeare and the Post Horses*, 1937.

H. B. Charlton, *Shakespearian Comedy*, 1938, pp. 193–8.

Peter Alexander, *Shakespeare, Life and Art*, 1938, pp. 124–7.

TO THE READER

The following is a brief description of the punctuation and other typographical devices employed in the text, which have been more fully explained in the *Note on Punctuation* and the *Textual Introduction* to be found in *The Tempest* volume:

An obelisk (†) implies corruption or emendation, and suggests a reference to the Notes.

A single bracket at the beginning of a speech signifies an 'aside.'

Four dots represent a full-stop in the original, except when it occurs at the end of a speech, and they mark a long pause.

Original colons or semicolons, which denote a somewhat shorter pause, are retained, or represented as three dots when they appear to possess special dramatic significance.

Similarly, significant commas have been given as dashes.

Round brackets are taken from the original, and mark a significant change of voice; when the original brackets seem to imply little more than the drop in tone accompanying parenthesis, they are conveyed by commas or dashes.

In plays for which both Folio and Quarto texts exist, passages taken from the text not selected as the basis for the present edition will be enclosed within square brackets.

Single inverted commas (' ') are editorial; double ones (" ") derive from the original, where they are used to draw attention to maxims, quotations, etc.

The reference number for the first line is given at the head of each page. Numerals in square brackets are placed at the beginning of the traditional acts and scenes.

THE MERRY WIVES
OF WINDSOR

The scene: Windsor

CHARACTERS IN THE PLAY

SIR JOHN FALSTAFF

FENTON, *a young gentleman*

ROBERT SHALLOW, *a country justice*

ABRAHAM SLENDER, *his wise cousin*

FRANK FORD } *two citizens of Windsor*
GEORGE PAGE }

WILLIAM PAGE, *a boy, son to Master Page*

SIR HUGH EVANS, *a Welsh parson*

DOCTOR CAIUS, *a French physician*

The Host of the Garter Inn

BARDOLPH }
PISTOL   } *irregular humorists, followers of Falstaff*
NYM   }

ROBIN, *page to Falstaff*

SIMPLE, *servant to Slender*

JOHN RUGBY, *servant to Doctor Caius*

JOHN   } *servants to Master Ford*
ROBERT }

MISTRESS FORD } *the merry wives*
MISTRESS PAGE }

ANNE PAGE, *her daughter, beloved of Fenton*

MISTRESS QUICKLY, *servant to Doctor Caius*

THE MERRY WIVES
OF WINDSOR

[I. I.] *A street in Windsor, before the house of Master Page*
Trees and a seat

Justice SHALLOW, SLENDER, and Sir HUGH EVANS
approach, holding lively conversation

Shallow [*hotly*]. Sir Hugh, persuade me not: I will make
a Star-chamber matter of it. If he were twenty Sir John
Falstaffs, he shall not abuse Robert Shallow, esquire.

Slender [*nodding*]. In the county of Gloucester, justice
of peace and 'Coram.'

Shallow. Ay, cousin Slender, and 'Custalorum.'

Slender. Ay, and 'Ratolorum' too; and a gentleman
born, master parson, who writes himself 'Armigero,' in
any bill, warrant, quittance, or obligation—'Armigero.'

Shallow. Ay, that I do, and have done any time these   10
three hundred years.

Slender. All his successors—gone before him—have
done't: and all his ancestors—that come after him—may...
They may give the dozen white luces in their coat.

Shallow [*proudly*]. It is an old coat.

Evans. The dozen white louses do become an old coat
well: it agrees well, passant: it is a familiar beast to man,
and signifies love.

Shallow [*coldly*]. The luce is the fresh fish—the salt fish
is an old †cod.   20

Slender. I may quarter, coz.

Shallow. You may—by marrying.

Evans. It is marring indeed, if he quarter it.

Shallow. Not a whit.

Evans. Yes, py'rlady: if he has a quarter of your coat,

there is but three skirts for yourself, in my simple conjectures; but that is all one...If Sir John Falstaff have committed disparagements unto you, I am of the Church, and will be glad to do my benevolence, to make atonements and compromises between you.

Shallow. The Council shall hear it! it is a riot.

Evans. It is not meet the council hear a riot: there is no fear of Got in a riot: the council, look you, shall desire to hear the fear of Got, and not to hear a riot: take your vizaments in that.

Shallow. Ha...o'my life, if I were young again, the sword should end it.

Evans. It is petter that friends is the swort, and end it: and there is also another device in my prain, which peradventure prings goot discretions with it....There is Anne Page, which is daughter to Master Thomas Page, which is pretty virginity.

Slender. Mistress Anne Page? She has brown hair, and speaks small like a woman.

Evans. It is that fery person for all the 'orld, as just as you will desire, and seven hundred pounds of moneys, and gold, and silver, is her grandsire, upon his death's-bed— Got deliver to a joyful resurrections!—give, when she is able to overtake seventeen years old....It were a goot motion if we leave our pribbles and prabbles, and desire a marriage between Master Abraham and Mistress Anne Page.

†*Shallow.* Did her grandsire leave her seven hundred pound?

Evans. Ay, and her father is make her a petter penny.

†*Shallow.* I know the young gentlewoman. She has good gifts.

Evans. Seven hundred pounds, and possibilities, is goot gifts.

Shallow. Well, let us see honest Master Page...Is Falstaff 60
there?

Evans. Shall I tell you a lie? I do despise a liar as I do
despise one that is false, or as I despise one that is not
true: the knight, Sir John, is there, and I beseech you be
ruled by your well-willers: I will peat the door for Master
Page....[*knocks and calls*] What, ho! Got-pless your
house here!

Page [*from within*]. Who's there?

Evans. Here is Got's plessing, and your friend, and
Justice Shallow, and here young Master Slender...that 70
peradventures shall tell you another tale, if matters grow
to your likings.

Page [*opens the door and comes out*]. I am glad to see your
worships well...I thank you for my venison, Master
Shallow.

Shallow. Master Page, I am glad to see you: much good
do it your good heart: I wished your venison better—it
was ill killed...How doth good Mistress Page?—and I
thank you always with my heart, la! with my heart.

Page. Sir, I thank you. 80

Shallow. Sir, I thank you: by yea and no, I do.

Page. I am glad to see you, good Master Slender.

Slender. How does your fallow greyhound, sir? I heard
say he was outrun on Cotsall.

Page. It could not be judged, sir.

Slender. You'll not confess...you'll not confess.

Shallow. That he will not. 'Tis your fault, 'tis your fault:
'tis a good dog.

Page. A cur, sir.

Shallow. Sir: he's a good dog, and a fair dog—can there be 90
more said? he is 'good and fair'....Is Sir John Falstaff here?

Page. Sir, he is within: and I would I could do a good
office between you.

Evans. It is spoke as a Christians ought to speak.

Shallow. He hath wronged me, Master Page.

Page. Sir, he doth in some sort confess it.

Shallow. If it be confessed, it is not redressed; is not that so, Master Page? He hath wronged me, indeed he hath, at a word he hath: believe me—Robert Shallow, esquire, saith he is wronged.

Page. Here comes Sir John.

Sir JOHN FALSTAFF, BARDOLPH, NYM, and PISTOL come from the house

Falstaff. Now, Master Shallow, you'll complain of me to the king?

Shallow. Knight, you have beaten my men, killed my deer, and broke open my lodge.

Falstaff. But not kissed your keeper's daughter!

Shallow. Tut, a pin! this shall be answered.

Falstaff. I will answer it straight. I have done all this... That is now answered.

Shallow. The Council shall know this.

Falstaff. 'Twere better for you, if it were known in counsel: you'll be laughed at.

Evans. Pauca verba; Sir John—goot worts.

Falstaff. Good worts! good cabbage...Slender, I broke your head: what matter have you against me?

Slender. Marry, sir, I have matter in my head against you, and against your cony-catching rascals, Bardolph, Nym, and Pistol. [They carried me to the tavern, and made me drunk, and afterward picked my pocket.]

Bardolph. You Banbury cheese!   [*he draws his sword*

Slender. Ay, it is no matter.

Pistol. How now, Mephostophilus!   [*he also draws*

Slender [*faintly*]. Ay, it is no matter.

Nym [pricks him with his sword]. Slice, I say; pauca, pauca: slice! that's my humour.

Slender [desperate]. Where's Simple, my man? can you tell, cousin?

Evans [comes between them]. Peace, I pray you...[*the three withdraw*] Now let us understand...[*takes out a note-book*] There is three umpires in this matter, as I under- 130 stand; [*writes*] that is, Master Page (fidelicet Master Page) and there is myself (fidelicet myself) and the three party is (lastly and finally) mine host of the Garter.

Page. We three, to hear it and end it between them.

Evans. Fery goot. I will make a prief of it in my note-book, and we will afterwards 'ork upon the cause, with as great discreetly as we can.   [*he writes again*

Falstaff. Pistol.

Pistol. He hears with ears.

Evans [looks up]. The tevil and his tam! what phrase is 140 this, 'He hears with ear'? why, it is affectations.

Falstaff. Pistol, did you pick Master Slender's purse?

Slender. Ay, by these gloves, did he—or I would I might never come in mine own great chamber again else—of seven groats in mill-sixpences, and two Edward shovel-boards, that cost me two shilling and two pence a-piece of Yed Miller...by these gloves!

Falstaff. Is this true, Pistol?

Evans. No, it is false, if it is a pick-purse.

Pistol. Ha, thou mountain-foreigner! Sir John, and
master mine,   150
I combat challenge of this latten bilbo:
Word of denial in thy labras here;
Word of denial; froth and scum, thou liest!

Slender. By these gloves, then 'twas he.
                                              [*pointing at Nym*

Nym. Be avised, sir, and pass good humours: I will say

'marry trap' with you, if you run the nuthook's humour on me—that is the very note of it.

Slender. By this hat, then he in the red face had it: for though I cannot remember what I did when you made me drunk, yet I am not altogether an ass.

Falstaff. What say you, Scarlet and John?

Bardolph. Why, sir, for my part, I say the gentleman had drunk himself out of his five sentences.

Evans. It is his five senses: fie, what the ignorance is!

Bardolph. And being †fap, sir, was, as they say, cashiered ...and so conclusions passed the careers.

Slender. Ay, you spake in Latin then too: but 'tis no matter; I'll ne'er be drunk whilst I live again, but in honest, civil, godly company, for this trick: if I be drunk, I'll be drunk with those that have the fear of God, and not with drunken knaves.

Evans. So Got-'udge me, that is a virtuous mind.

Falstaff. You hear all these matters denied, gentlemen; you hear it.

During this talk ANNE PAGE, *bearing wine, comes from the house, with Mistress* PAGE *and Mistress* FORD

Page. Nay daughter, carry the wine in—we'll drink within.   [*she obeys*

Slender. O heaven...this is Mistress Anne Page!

Page. How now, Mistress Ford!

Falstaff. Mistress Ford, by my troth, you are very well met: by your leave, good mistress.   ['*kisses her*'

Page. Wife, bid these gentlemen welcome...Come, we have a hot venison pasty to dinner; come, gentlemen, I hope we shall drink down all unkindness.

[*all but Slender enter the house*

Slender. I had rather than forty shillings I had my Book of Songs and Sonnets here...

SIMPLE comes up the street

How now Simple, where have you been? I must wait on myself, must I? You have not the Book of Riddles about you, have you?

Simple. Book of Riddles? why, did you not lend it to Alice Shortcake upon Allhallowmas last, a fortnight afore 190 Michaelmas?

SHALLOW and EVANS return to look for SLENDER

Shallow. Come coz, come coz, we stay for you...[*taking him by the arm*] A word with you, coz...marry, this, coz... there is as 'twere a tender, a kind of tender, made afar off by Sir Hugh here...Do you understand me?

Slender. Ay, sir, you shall find me reasonable; if it be so, I shall do that that is reason.

Shallow. Nay, but understand me.

Slender. So I do, sir.

Evans [*at his other side*]. Give ear to his motions; Master 200 Slender, I will description the matter to you, if you be capacity of it.

Slender. Nay, I will do as my cousin Shallow says: I pray you pardon me—he's a justice of peace in his country, simple though I stand here.

Evans. But that is not the question: the question is concerning your marriage.

Shallow. Ay, there's the point, sir.

Evans. Marry, is it: the very point of it—to Mistress Anne Page. 210

Slender. Why, if it be so...I will marry her upon any reasonable demands.

Evans. But can you affection the 'oman? Let us command to know that of your mouth, or of your lips: for divers philosophers hold that the lips is parcel of the

M.W.W. – 4

mouth: therefore, precisely, can you carry your good will to the maid?

Shallow. Cousin Abraham Slender, can you love her?

Slender. I hope, sir, I will do as it shall become one that
220 would do reason.

Evans. Nay, Got's lords and his ladies! you must speak possitable, if you can carry-her your desires towards her.

Shallow. That you must...Will you—upon good dowry— marry her?

Slender. I will do a greater thing than that, upon your request, cousin, in any reason.

Shallow. Nay, conceive me, conceive me, sweet coz: what I do is to pleasure you, coz: can you love the maid?

Slender. I will marry her, sir, at your request; but if
230 there be no great love in the beginning, yet heaven may decrease it upon better acquaintance, when we are married and have more occasion to know one another: I hope upon familiarity will grow more contempt: but if you say, 'marry her,' I will marry her—that I am freely dissolved, and dissolutely.

Evans. It is a fery discretion-answer; save the fall is in the 'ort 'dissolutely': the 'ort is, according to our mean- ing, 'resolutely': his meaning is goot.

Shallow. Ay...I think my cousin meant well.

240 *Slender.* Ay, or else I would I might be hanged, la!

ANNE PAGE *returns*

Shallow. Here comes fair Mistress Anne; [*he bows*] Would I were young for your sake, Mistress Anne!

Anne [*curtsies*]. The dinner is on the table. My father desires your worships' company.

Shallow. I will wait on him, fair Mistress Anne.

Evans [*hurries in*]. Od's plessed-will...I will not be absence at the grace.   [*Shallow follows*

Anne [*to Slender*]. Will't please your worship to come in, sir?

Slender [*simpering*]. No—I thank you forsooth—heartily; 250 I am very well.

Anne. The dinner attends you, sir.

Slender. I am not a-hungry, I thank you, forsooth…[*to Simple*] Go, sirrah, for all you are my man, go wait upon my cousin Shallow…[*Simple goes in*] A justice of peace sometime may be beholding to his friend, for a man; I keep but three men and a boy yet, till my mother be dead: but what though? yet I live like a poor gentleman born.

Anne. I may not go in without your worship: they will 260 not sit till you come.

Slender. I'faith, I'll eat nothing: I thank you as much as though I did.

Anne [*impatient*]. I pray you sir walk in.

Slender. I had rather walk here—I thank you. I bruised my shin th'other day with playing at sword and dagger with a master of fence—three veneys for a dish of stewed prunes—[and I with my ward defending my head, he hot my shin,] and, by my troth, I cannot abide the smell of hot meat since….Why do your dogs bark so? be there 270 bears i'th' town?

Anne. I think there are, sir. I heard them talked of.

Slender. I love the sport well, but I shall as soon quarrel at it as any man in England…You are afraid, if you see the bear loose, are you not?

Anne. Ay, indeed, sir.

Slender. That's meat and drink to me, now: I have seen Sackerson loose—twenty times, and have taken him by the chain: but, I warrant you, the women have so cried and shrieked at it, that it passed…But women, indeed, 280 cannot abide 'em—they are very ill-favoured rough things.

PAGE opens the door

Page. Come, gentle Master Slender, come; we stay for you.

Slender. I'll eat nothing, I thank you, sir.

Page. By cock and pie, you shall not choose, sir: come, come!   [*he stands aside to let him pass in*

Slender. Nay, pray you lead the way.

Page [*going in*]. Come on, sir.

Slender [*begins to follow but then turns*]. Mistress Anne...
290 yourself shall go first.

Anne. Not I, sir! pray you keep on.

Slender. Truly, I will not go first: truly, la! I will not do you that wrong.

Anne [*keeps behind him*]. I pray you, sir.

Slender. I'll rather be unmannerly than troublesome: you do yourself wrong, indeed, la!

He goes in; she follows after

[I. 2.]   *Sir HUGH EVANS and SIMPLE appear
at the door*

Evans. Go your ways, and ask of Doctor Caius' house which is the way; and there dwells one Mistress Quickly; which is in the manner of his nurse—or his dry nurse— or his cook—or his laundry—his washer and his wringer.

Simple. Well, sir.

Evans. Nay, it is petter yet...Give her this letter; for it is a 'oman, that altogether's acquaintance with Mistress Anne Page; and the letter is to desire and require her to solicit your master's desires to Mistress Anne Page: I pray
10 you, be gone...I will make an end of my dinner; there's pippins and seese to come.

SIMPLE departs; EVANS goes within

[1. 3.] *A room in the Garter Inn, hung with arras; stairs leading to a gallery. FALSTAFF seated at a table, drinking: HOST busy with mugs and pewter cans: PISTOL, NYM, BARDOLPH and ROBIN*

Falstaff [*sets down his cup of sack*]. Mine host of the Garter!

Host [*turns*]. What says my bully-rook? speak scholarly and wisely.

Falstaff. Truly, mine host; I must turn away some of my followers.

Host. Discard, bully Hercules, cashier; let them wag; trot, trot.

Falstaff. I sit at ten pounds a week.

Host. Thou'rt an emperor—Cæsar, Keisar, and Pheazar. 10 I will entertain Bardolph: he shall draw; he shall tap; said I well, bully Hector?

Falstaff. Do so, good mine host.

Host. I have spoke: let him follow...[*to Bardolph*] Let me see thee froth and lime: I am at a word: follow.

[*he goes out*

Falstaff. Bardolph, follow him: a tapster is a good trade: an old cloak makes a new jerkin: a withered serving-man a fresh tapster...Go, adieu.

Bardolph. It is a life that I have desired: I will thrive.

Pistol. O base Hungarian wight: wilt thou the spigot 20 wield? [*Bardolph follows Host*

Nym. He was gotten in drink. [His mind is not heroic, and there's the humour of it]...Is not the humour conceited?

Falstaff. I am glad I am so acquit of this tinderbox: his thefts were too open: his filching was like an unskilful singer, he kept not time.

Nym. The good humour is to steal at a †minim-rest.

Pistol. 'Convey,' the wise it call...'Steal!' foh! a fico
30 for the phrase.

Falstaff. Well, sirs, I am almost out at heels.

Pistol. Why, then, let kibes ensue.

Falstaff. There is no remedy: I must cony-catch, I must shift.

Pistol. Young ravens must have food.

Falstaff. Which of you know Ford of this town?

Pistol. I ken the wight: he is of substance good.

Falstaff. My honest lads, I will tell you what I am about.

Pistol. Two yards, and more.

40 *Falstaff.* No quips now, Pistol...Indeed, I am in the waist two yards about: but I am now about no waste: I am about thrift—Briefly: I do mean to make love to Ford's wife: I spy entertainment in her: she discourses: she carves: she gives the leer of invitation...I can construe the action of her familiar style, and the hardest voice of her behaviour—to be Englished rightly—is, 'I am Sir John Falstaff's.'

Pistol. He hath studied her †well, and translated her will...out of honesty into English.

50 *Nym.* The anchor is deep: will that humour pass?

Falstaff. Now, the report goes she has all the rule of her husband's purse: he hath a legion of angels.

Pistol. As many devils entertain! and 'To her, Boy,' say I.

Nym. The humour rises: it is good: humour me the angels.

Falstaff. I have writ me here a letter to her: and here another to Page's wife; who even now gave me good eyes too; examined my parts with most judicious œillades:
60 sometimes the beam of her view gilded my foot...sometimes my portly belly.

Pistol. Then did the sun on dunghill shine.

Nym. I thank thee for that humour.

Falstaff. O, she did so course o'er my exteriors with such a greedy intention, that the appetite of her eye did seem to scorch me up like a burning-glass...Here's another letter to her: she bears the purse too: she is a region in Guiana: all gold and bounty...I will be cheaters to them both, and they shall be exchequers to me: they shall be my East and West Indies, and I will trade to them both... 70 [*to Pistol*] Go, bear thou this letter to Mistress Page; [*to Nym*] and thou this to Mistress Ford: we will thrive, lads, we will thrive.

Pistol. Shall I Sir Pandarus of Troy become—
And by my side wear steel! then, Lucifer take all!

Nym. I will run no base humour: here, take the humour-letter; I will keep the haviour of reputation.
                              [*they throw the letters on the table*
Falstaff [*rising, to Robin*]. Hold, sirrah, bear you these letters tightly,
Sail like my pinnace to these golden shores....
Rogues, hence, avaunt, vanish like hail-stones; go!
Trudge; plod away i'th' hoof; seek shelter, pack...   80
Falstaff will learn the humour of this age,
French thrift, you rogues—myself and skirted page!
                              [*he sweeps out, with Robin following*
Pistol. Let vultures gripe thy guts: for gourd and fullam holds,
And high and low beguiles the rich and poor:
Tester I'll have in pouch when thou shalt lack,
Base Phrygian Turk!

Nym. I have operations [in my head] which be humours of revenge.

Pistol. Wilt thou revenge?

Nym.   By welkin and her star!   90

Pistol. With wit or steel?

Nym.   With both the humours, I:
I will discuss the humour of this love to Page.
Pistol. And I to Ford shall eke unfold,
          How Falstaff, varlet vile,
          His dove will prove, his gold will hold,
          And his soft couch defile.
Nym. My humour shall not cool: I will incense Page to
deal with poison: I will possess him with' †yellows, for the
revolt of †mind is dangerous: that is my true humour.
100   *Pistol.* Thou art the Mars of malcontents: I second thee:
troop on.   [*they go*

[1. 4.] *A room in Doctor Caius' house: tables and shelves
covered with books, papers, bottles, retorts etc.; a door at the
back opening into a small closet; two other doors, one leading
to the street, with a window beside it*

Mistress QUICKLY: SIMPLE

Quickly [*calling*]. What, John Rugby!

RUGBY *enters*

I pray thee, go to the casement, and see if you can see my
master, Master Doctor Caius, coming: if he do, i'faith,
and find any body in the house...here will be an old
abusing of God's patience and the king's English.
Rugby. I'll go watch.
Quickly. Go, and we'll have a posset for't soon at night,
in faith at the latter end of a sea-coal fire...[*Rugby goes to
the window*] An honest, willing, kind fellow, as ever servant
10 shall come in house withal: and, I warrant you, no tell-
tale nor no breed-bate: his worst fault is, that he is given
to prayer; he is something peevish that way: but nobody
but has his fault: but let that pass....Peter Simple, you
say your name is?

Simple. Ay...for fault of a better.

Quickly. And Master Slender's your master?

Simple. Ay, forsooth.

Quickly. Does he not wear a great round beard, like a glover's paring-knife?

Simple. No, forsooth: he hath but a little †whey-face; 20 with a little yellow beard...a cane-coloured beard.

Quickly. A softly-sprighted man, is he not?

Simple. Ay, forsooth: but he is as tall a man of his hands as any is between this and his head: he hath fought with a warrener!

Quickly. How say you?—O, I should remember him: does he not hold up his head, as it were, and strut in his gait?

Simple. Yes, indeed, does he.

Quickly. Well, heaven send Anne Page no worse fortune ...Tell Master Parson Evans I will do what I can for your 30 master: Anne is a good girl, and I wish—

Rugby [*calls from the window*]. Out, alas! here comes my master.

Quickly. We shall all be shent...Run in here, good young man: go into this closet...[*she shuts Simple in the closet*] He will not stay long...[*calling*] What, John Rugby! John! what, John, I say!

      CAIUS enters; she feigns not to see him

Go, John, go enquire for my master. I doubt he be not well, that he comes not home...   [*she sings*

      And down, down, adown-a, &c.   40

Caius [*suspicious*]. Vat is you sing? I do not like des toys: pray you, go and vetch me in my closet un boitier vert; a box, a green-a box...[*testily*] Do intend vat I speak? a green-a box.   [*he busies himself with papers*

Quickly. Ay, forsooth, I'll fetch it you...[*to Rugby*] I am glad he went not in himself: if he had found the young man, he would have been horn-mad. [*she goes to the closet*

Caius [*wipes his forehead*]. Fe, fe, fe, fe! ma foi, il fait fort chaud. Je m'en vais à la cour—la grande affaire.

50 *Quickly* [*returning with a green case*]. Is it this, sir?

Caius. Oui, mette le au mon pocket, dépêche Quickly... Vere is dat knave Rugby?

Quickly. What, John Rugby! John!

Rugby [*comes forward*]. Here, sir.

Caius. You are John Rugby, and you are Jack Rugby... Come, tak-a your rapier, and come after my heel to de court.

Rugby [*opening the door*]. 'Tis ready, sir, here in the porch.

60 *Caius* [*following swiftly*]. By my trot: I tarry too long ...[*stops*] Od's me...Qu'ai-j'oublié! [*rushes to the closet*] dere is some simples in my closet, dat I vill not for the varld I shall leave behind.

Quickly. Ay me, he'll find the young man there, and be mad.

Caius [*discovers Simple*]. O diable, diable! vat is in my closet? Villainy! laroon! [*pulling him out*] Rugby, my rapier.

Quickly. Good master, be content.

70 *Caius*. Verefore shall I be content-a?

Quickly. The young man is an honest man.

Caius. Vat shall de honest man do in my closet? dere is no honest man dat shall come in my closet.

Quickly. I beseech you, be not so phlegmatic: hear the truth of it....He came of an errand to me from Parson Hugh.

Caius. Vell.

Simple. Ay, forsooth...to desire her to—

Quickly. Peace, I pray you.

80 *Caius*. Peac-a your tongue...Speak-a your tale.

Simple. To desire this honest gentlewoman, your maid,

to speak a good word to Mistress Anne Page—for my
master in the way of marriage.

Quickly. This is all, indeed, la! but I'll ne'er put my
finger in the fire, and need not.

Caius. Sir Hugh send-a you! Rugby, baillez me some
paper...tarry you a littl-a while.

[*he sits at his desk and writes*

Quickly [*draws Simple aside*]. I am glad he is so quiet:
if he had been throughly moved, you should have heard
him so loud, and so melancholy...But notwithstanding,   90
man, I'll do your master what good I can: and the very
yea and the no is, the French doctor, my master—I may
call him my master, look you, for I keep his house; and
I wash, wring, brew, bake, scour, dress meat and drink,
make the beds, and do all myself—

Simple. 'Tis a great charge to come under one body's
hand.

Quickly. Are you avised o'that? you shall find it a great
charge: and to be up early, and down late...but notwithstanding (to tell you in your ear, I would have no words   100
of it) my master himself is in love with Mistress Anne
Page: but notwithstanding that I know Anne's mind,
that's neither here nor there.

Caius [*rising and folding the letter*]. You, jack'nape! giv-a
this letter to Sir Hugh. By gar, it is a shallenge: I vill
cut his troat in de Park, and I vill teach a scurvy jack-a-
nape priest to meddle or make!—You may be gone: it is
not good you tarry here...[*Simple goes*] By gar, I vill cut
all his two stones: by gar, he shall not have a stone to
trow at his dog.   110

Quickly. Alas: he speaks but for his friend.

Caius [*turns upon her*]. It is no matter-a ver dat: do
not you tell-a me dat I shall have Anne Page for myself?
By gar, I vill kill de Jack-priest...and I have appointed

mine host of de Jarteer to measure our weapon...by gar,
I vill myself have Anne Page.

Quickly. Sir, the maid loves you, and all shall be well:
We must give folks leave to prate...[*he boxes her ears*]
What the good-jer!   [*rubbing her head*
120 *Caius.* ·Rugby, come to the court vit me...[*to Quickly*]
By gar, if I have not Anne Page, I shall turn your head
out of my door...Follow my heels, Rugby.

          Snatching up his green case and simples,
            he hurries out, followed by Rugby

Quickly. You shall have An—[*the door shuts*]—fool's-head
of your own...No, I know Anne's mind for that: never
a woman in Windsor knows more of Anne's mind than
I do, nor can do more than I do with her, I thank heaven.
Fenton [*from outside*]. Who's within there, ho!
Quickly. Who's there, I trow? Come near the house,
I pray you.

          FENTON opens the door and enters

130 *Fenton.* How now, good woman, how dost thou?
Quickly. The better that it pleases your good worship
to ask.
Fenton. What news? how does pretty Mistress Anne?
Quickly. In truth, sir, and she is pretty, and honest,
and gentle, and one that is your friend, I can tell you that
by the way, I praise heaven for it.
Fenton. Shall I do any good, think'st thou? Shall I not
lose my suit?
Quickly. Troth, sir, all is in his hands above: but not-
140 withstanding, Master Fenton, I'll be sworn on a book
she loves you...Have not your worship a wart above
your eye?
Fenton. Yes marry have I, what of that?
Quickly. Well, thereby hangs a tale...good faith, it is

such another Nan; but—I detest—an honest maid as ever broke bread...We had an hour's talk of that wart; I shall never laugh but in that maid's company...but, indeed, she is given too much to allicholy and musing...But for you—well—go to—

Fenton. Well...I shall see her to-day: hold, there's money   150
for thee...Let me have thy voice in my behalf: if thou seest her before me, commend me—

Quickly. Will I? i'faith, that we will: and I will tell your worship more of the wart the next time we have confidence, and of other wooers.

Fenton. Well, farewell. I am in great haste now.

[he goes out

Quickly. Farewell to your worship...Truly, an honest gentleman: but Anne loves him not: for I know Anne's mind as well as another does...Out upon't! what have I forgot?   *[she hurries away*   160

[2. 1.] *The street before the house of Master Page*
Mistress PAGE, in hat and muffler, comes forth
with a letter in her hand

Mistress Page. What, have I 'scaped love-letters in the holiday time of my beauty, and am I now a subject for them? Let me see!   *[she reads*
'Ask me no reason why I love you, for though Love use Reason for his precisian, he admits him not for his councillor...You are not young, no more am I: go to then, there's sympathy...you are merry, so am I: ha! ha! then there's more sympathy...you love sack, and so do I: would you desire better sympathy? Let it suffice thee, Mistress Page, at the least if the love of a soldier can suffice, that   10
I love thee: I will not say, pity me—'tis not a soldier-like phrase; but I say, love me...

By me, thine own true knight, by day or night:
Or any kind of light, with all his might,
For thee to fight.

JOHN FALSTAFF.'

What a Herod of Jewry is this! O wicked, wicked world!
One that is well-nigh worn to pieces with age to show
himself a young gallant! What an unweighed behaviour
20 hath this Flemish drunkard picked (with the devil's name!)
out of my conversation, that he dares in this manner
assay me? Why, he hath not been thrice in my company:
what should I say to him? I was then frugal of my
mirth...Heaven forgive me! Why, I'll exhibit a bill in
the parliament for the putting down of men...How shall
I be revenged on him? for revenged I will be!—as sure
as his guts are made of puddings.

Mistress FORD appears, walking towards Page's house

Mistress Ford. Mistress Page! trust me, I was going to
your house.
30 *Mistress Page.* And, trust me, I was coming to you...
You look very ill.
Mistress Ford. Nay, I'll ne'er believe that; I have to
show to the contrary.
Mistress Page. Faith, but you do, in my mind.
Mistress Ford. Well: I do then: yet, I say, I could show
you to the contrary...O Mistress Page, give me some
counsel!
Mistress Page. What's the matter, woman?
Mistress Ford. O woman...if it were not for one trifling
40 respect, I could come to such honour.
Mistress Page. Hang the trifle, woman, take the honour:
what is it? Dispense with trifles: what is it?
Mistress Ford. If I would but go to hell for an eternal
moment or so...I could be knighted!

Mistress Page. What? thou liest! Sir Alice Ford! These knights will hack, and so thou shouldst not alter the article of thy gentry.

Mistress Ford. We burn day-light…[*hands her a letter*] Here, read, read: perceive how I might be knighted. I shall think the worse of fat men, as long as I have an eye 50 to make difference of men's liking: and yet he would not swear; praised women's modesty; and gave such orderly and well-behaved reproof to all uncomeliness, that I would have sworn his disposition would have gone to the truth of his words: but they do no more adhere and keep place together than the Hundredth Psalm to the tune of 'Green-sleeves'…What tempest, I trow, threw this whale, with so many tuns of oil in his belly, ashore at Windsor? How shall I be revenged on him? I think the best way were to entertain him with hope, till the wicked fire of lust have 60 melted him in his own grease…Did you ever hear the like?

Mistress Page [*holding the two letters, side by side*]. Letter for letter; but that the name of Page and Ford differs… To thy great comfort in this mystery of ill opinions, here's the twin-brother of thy letter: but let thine inherit first, for I protest mine never shall: I warrant he hath a thousand of these letters, writ with blank space for different names—sure more!—and these are of the second edition: he will print them out of doubt; for he cares not what he puts into the press, when he would put us two… 70 I had rather be a giantess, and lie under Mount Pelion… Well; I will find you twenty lascivious turtles ere one chaste man.

Mistress Ford [*taking Mistress Page's letter*]. Why, this is the very same…the very hand…the very words! What doth he think of us?

Mistress Page. Nay, I know not: it makes me almost ready to wrangle with mine own honesty: I'll entertain

myself like one that I am not acquainted withal; for, sure,
80 unless he know some strain in me, that I know not myself,
he would never have boarded me in this fury.

Mistress Ford. 'Boarding,' call you it? I'll be sure to
keep him above deck.

Mistress Page. So will I: if he come under my hatches,
I'll never to sea again...Let's be revenged on him: let's
appoint him a meeting; give him a show of comfort in
his suit, and lead him on with a fine-baited delay, till he
hath pawned his horses to mine host of the Garter.

Mistress Ford. Nay, I will consent to act any villainy
90 against him, that may not sully the chariness of our
honesty...O, that my husband saw this letter: it would
give eternal food to his jealousy.

Mistress Page. Why, look where he comes; and my good
man too: he's as far from jealousy, as I am from giving
him cause—and that, I hope, is an unmeasurable distance.

Mistress Ford. You are the happier woman.

Mistress Page. Let's consult together against this greasy
knight...Come hither.

They seat themselves unseen under the trees, within earshot:
FORD and PISTOL, PAGE and NYM come up in pairs, talking

Ford. Well...I hope it be not so.
100 *Pistol.* Hope is a curtal-dog in some affairs:
Sir John affects thy wife.

Ford. Why, sir, my wife is not young.

Pistol. He wooes both high and low, both rich and poor,
Both young and old, one with another, Ford.
He loves the gallimaufry—Ford, perpend.

Ford. Love my wife!

Pistol. With liver burning hot: prevent...or go thou,
†Like Sir Actæon be, with Ringwood at thy heels...
O, odious is the name!

Ford. What name, sir?   110

Pistol. The horn, I say...Farewell...

Take heed, have open eye, for thieves do foot by night....

Take heed, ere summer comes or cuckoo-birds do sing....

†Away, Sir Corporal Nym...[*to Page*] Believe it, he
   speaks sense.   [*Pistol swaggers off*

(*Ford.* I will be patient...I will find out this.

Nym [*to Page*]. And this is true: I like not the humour
of lying: he hath wronged me in some humours: I should
have borne the humoured letter to her: but I have a
sword: and it shall bite upon my necessity: he loves your
wife; there's the short and the long...   120

My name is Corporal Nym: I speak, and I avouch;

'Tis true: my name is Nym: and Falstaff loves
   your wife

...Adieu. I love not the humour of bread and cheese,
[and there's the humour of it]...Adieu.

       [*he follows Pistol; Page and Ford muse apart*

Page. 'The humour of it,' quoth 'a! here's a fellow frights
English out of his wits.

Ford. I will seek out Falstaff.

Page. I never heard such a drawling, affecting rogue.

Ford. If I do find it...well.

Page. I will not believe such a Cataian, though the   130
priest o'th' town commended him for a true man.

Ford. 'Twas a good sensible fellow...well.

   Mistress PAGE *and Mistress* FORD *come forward,*
            having heard all

Page. How now, Meg!

Mistress Page. Whither go you, George? Hark you.

                [*they speak together*

Mistress Ford [*demure*]. How now, sweet Frank! why
art thou melancholy?

   M.W.W. – 5

Ford [*starts*]. I melancholy? I am not melancholy...Get you home: go.   [*he turns away*

Mistress Ford. Faith, thou hast some crotchets in thy
140 head now...Will you go, Mistress Page?

Mistress Page. Have with you....You'll come to dinner, George? [*in Mistress Ford's ear*] Look, who comes yonder: she shall be our messenger to this paltry knight.

Mistress Ford. Trust me, I thought on her: she'll fit it.

Mistress QUICKLY comes up

Mistress Page. You are come to see my daughter Anne?

Quickly. Ay, forsooth: and, I pray, how does good Mistress Anne?

Mistress Page. Go in with us and see: we have an hour's talk with you.   [*they go within*

150 *Page.* How now, Master Ford!

Ford [*rouses*]. You heard what this knave told me, did you not?

Page. Yes, and you heard what the other told me?

Ford. Do you think there is truth in them?

Page. Hang 'em, slaves: I do not think the knight would offer it: but these that accuse him in his intent towards our wives are a yoke of his discarded men...very rogues, now they be out of service.

Ford. Were they his men?

160 *Page.* Marry, were they.

Ford. I like it never the better for that. Does he lie at the Garter?

Page. Ay, marry, does he...If he should intend this voyage towards my wife, I would turn her loose to him; and what he gets more of her than sharp words, let it lie on my head.

Ford. I do not misdoubt my wife...but I would be loath to turn them together...a man may be too confident...I

would have nothing lie on my head...I cannot be thus
satisfied.   170

> *HOST approaches in haste; SHALLOW following*
> *at a distance*

Page. Look where my ranting host of the Garter comes:
there is either liquor in his pate, or money in his purse,
when he looks so merrily...How now, mine host!

Host. How now, bully-rook! thou'rt a gentleman. [*turns
and calls*] Cavaliero-justice, I say!

Shallow [*breathless*]. I follow, mine host, I follow....
Good even and twenty, good Master Page! Master Page,
will you go with us? we have sport in hand.

Host. Tell him, cavaliero-justice: tell him, bully-rook.

Shallow. Sir, there is a fray to be fought, between Sir   180
Hugh the Welsh priest and Caius the French doctor.

Ford. Good mine host o'th' Garter...a word with you.

Host. What sayst thou, my bully-rook?

> [*they talk together apart*

Shallow [*to Page*]. Will you go with us to behold it? My
merry host hath had the measuring of their weapons;
and, I think, hath appointed them contrary places: for,
believe me, I hear the parson is no jester: hark, I will
tell you what our sport shall be.

> [*they talk together apart*

Host. Hast thou no suit against my knight, my guest-
cavalier?   190

†*Ford.* None, I protest: but I'll give you a pottle of
burnt sack to give me recourse to him, and tell him my
name is Brook...only for a jest.

Host. My hand, bully: thou shalt have egress and regress—said I well?—and thy name shall be Brook....It is
a merry knight: Will you go, †Ameers?   [*going*

Shallow. Have with you, mine host.

Page. I have heard the Frenchman hath good skill in his rapier.

200 *Shallow.* Tut, sir! I could have told you more: in these times you stand on distance...your passes, stoccadoes, and I know not what...'tis the heart, Master Page—'tis here, 'tis here: I have seen the time, with my long sword I would have made you four tall fellows skip like rats.

Host [*calling*]. Here, boys, here, here! shall we wag?

Page. Have with you...I had rather hear them scold than fight.   [*Shallow and Page follow Host*

Ford. Though Page be a secure fool, and stands so firmly on his wife's frailty—yet I cannot put off my

210 opinion so easily: she was in his company at Page's house...and, what they made there, I know not....Well, I will look further into't, and I have a disguise to sound Falstaff...If I find her honest, I lose not my labour: if she be otherwise, 'tis labour well bestowed.   [*he goes*

[2. 2.]   *The room in the Garter Inn*

FALSTAFF: PISTOL

[*Pistol.* I will retort the sum in equipage.]

Falstaff. I will not lend thee a penny.

Pistol. Why, then the world's mine oyster,
Which I with sword will open.

Falstaff. Not a penny: I have been content, sir, you should lay my countenance to pawn: I have grated upon my good friends for three reprieves for you and your coach-fellow, Nym; or else you had looked through the grate, like a geminy of baboons: I am damned in hell for

10 swearing to gentlemen my friends, you were good soldiers and tall fellows....and when Mistress Bridget lost the handle of her fan, I took't upon mine honour thou hadst it not.

Pistol. Didst thou not share? hadst thou not fifteen
　　pence?

Falstaff. Reason, you rogue, reason: think'st thou I'll
endanger my soul gratis? At a word, hang no more about
me, I am no gibbet for you...Go—a short knife and a
throng—to your manor of Pickt-hatch...Go. You'll not
bear a letter for me, you rogue! you stand upon your
honour! why, thou unconfinable baseness, it is as much
as I can do, to keep the terms of my honour precise...Ay, 20
ay, I myself sometimes, leaving the fear of God on the
left hand, and hiding mine honour in my necessity, am
fain to shuffle, to hedge, and to lurch—and yet you, rogue,
will ensconce your rags, your cat-a-mountain looks, your
red-lattice phrases, and your †bold-beating oaths, under
the shelter of your honour! You will not do it? you!

Pistol. I do relent: what wouldst thou more of man?

ROBIN *enters*

Robin. Sir, here's a woman would speak with you.
Falstaff. Let her approach.

Mistress QUICKLY *enters simpering:* ROBIN *and* PISTOL *converse apart*

Quickly [*curtsies*]. Give your worship good-morrow. 30
Falstaff. Good-morrow, good wife.
Quickly. Not so, an't please your worship.
Falstaff. Good maid, then.
Quickly. I'll be sworn,
As my mother was, the first hour I was born.
Falstaff. I do believe the swearer; what with me?
Quickly. Shall I vouchsafe your worship a word or
two?
Falstaff. Two thousand—fair woman—and I'll vouch-
safe thee the hearing. 40

Quickly. There is one Mistress Ford—[*glances round at Pistol and Robin*] Sir, I pray, come a little nearer this ways...I myself dwell with Master Doctor Caius...

Falstaff. Well, on; Mistress Ford, you say—

Quickly. Your worship says very true: I pray your worship, come a little nearer this ways.

Falstaff. I warrant thee, nobody hears: [*waves his hand towards Pistol and Robin*] mine own people, mine own people.

50   *Quickly.* Are they so? God bless them, and make them his servants!

Falstaff. Well; Mistress Ford, what of her?

Quickly. Why, sir; she's a good creature; Lord, Lord! your worship's a wanton...well...God forgive you, and all of us, I pray—

Falstaff. Mistress Ford...come, Mistress Ford.

Quickly. Marry, this is the short and the long of it: you have brought her into such a canaries, as 'tis wonderful: the best courtier of them all (when the court lay at
60   Windsor) could never have brought her to such a canary: yet there has been knights, and lords, and gentlemen, with their coaches; I warrant you, coach after coach, letter after letter, gift after gift; smelling so sweetly, all musk, and so rushling, I warrant you, in silk and gold, and in such alligant terms, and in such wine and sugar of the best, and the fairest, that would have won any woman's heart: and, I warrant you, they could never get an eye-wink of her: I had myself twenty angels given me this morning, but I defy all angels—in any such sort, as
70   they say—but in the way of honesty: and, I warrant you, they could never get her so much as sip on a cup with the proudest of them all, and yet there has been earls... nay, which is more, pensioners—but, I warrant you, all is one with her.

Falstaff. But what say, she to me? be brief, my good she-Mercury.

Quickly. Marry, she hath received your letter: for the which she thanks you a thousand times; and she gives you to notify that her husband will be absence from his house between ten and eleven.   80

Falstaff. Ten and eleven.

Quickly. Ay, forsooth: and then you may come and see the picture, she says, that you wot of: Master Ford, her husband, will be from home: alas! the sweet woman leads an ill life with him: he's a very jealousy man; she leads a very frampold life with him—good heart!

Falstaff. Ten and eleven....Woman, commend me to her. I will not fail her.

Quickly. Why, you say well...But I have another messenger to your worship: Mistress Page hath her hearty   90 commendations to you, too: and let me tell you in your ear, she's as fartuous a civil modest wife, and one, I tell you, that will not miss you morning nor evening prayer, as any is in Windsor, whoe'er be the other: and she bade me tell your worship that her husband is seldom from home, but she hopes there will come a time....I never knew a woman so dote upon a man; surely, I think you have charms, la...yes, in truth.

Falstaff. Not I, I assure thee; setting the attraction of my good parts aside, I have no other charms.   100

Quickly. Blessing on your heart for't!

Falstaff. But I pray thee tell me this: has Ford's wife, and Page's wife, acquainted each other how they love me?

Quickly. That were a jest, indeed! they have not so little grace, I hope—that were a trick, indeed! But Mistress Page would desire you to send her your little page, of all loves: her husband has a marvellous infection to the little page: and, truly, Master Page is an honest

man: never a wife in Windsor leads a better life than she
110 does: do what she will, say what she will, take all, pay
all, go to bed when she list, rise when she list, all is as
she will: and, truly, she deserves it; for if there be a kind
woman in Windsor, she is one: you must send her your
page—no remedy.

Falstaff. Why, I will.

Quickly. Nay, but do so then—and, look you, he may
come and go between you both: and, in any case, have
a nay-word, that you may know one another's mind, and
the boy never need to understand any thing; for 'tis not
120 good that children should know any wickedness: old folks,
you know, have discretion, as they say, and know the
world.

Falstaff. Fare thee well. Commend me to them both:
there's my purse—I am yet thy debtor...Boy, go along
with this woman. [*Quickly and Robin go out*] This news
distracts me....

(*Pistol.* †This pink is one of Cupid's carriers—
Clap on more sails, pursue: up with your fights:
Give fire: she is my prize, or ocean whelm them all!

[*he pursues them*

130 *Falstaff.* Sayst thou so, old Jack? go thy ways: I'll make
more of thy old body than I have done: will they yet
look after thee? wilt thou, after the expense of so much
money, be now a gainer? Good body, I thank thee: let
them say 'tis grossly done—so it be fairly done, no matter.

BARDOLPH enters, with a cup of sack

Bardolph. Sir John, there's one Master Brook below
would fain speak with you, and be acquainted with you;
and hath sent your worship a morning's draught of sack.

Falstaff. Brook is his name?

Bardolph. Ay, sir.

Falstaff. Call him in...[*Bardolph goes out*] Such Brooks 140
are welcome to me, that o'erflow such liquor...[*he drains
the cup*] Ah, ha! Mistress Ford and Mistress Page, have
I encompassed you? go to, via!

> *BARDOLPH returns, with FORD disguised carrying
> a bag of money*

Ford. Bless you, sir.

Falstaff. And you, sir: would you speak with me?

Ford. I make bold, to press with so little preparation
upon you.

Falstaff. You're welcome. What's your will? Give us
leave, drawer.   [*Bardolph leaves them*

Ford. Sir, I am a gentleman that have spent much. 150
My name is Brook.

Falstaff. Good Master Brook, I desire more acquaintance of you.

Ford. Good Sir John, I sue for yours: not to charge
you, for I must let you understand I think myself in
better plight for a lender than you are: the which hath
something emboldened me to this unseasoned intrusion:
for they say, if money go before, all ways do lie open.

Falstaff. Money is a good soldier, sir, and will on.

Ford. Troth, and I have a bag of money here troubles 160
me: if you will help me to bear it, Sir John, take all, or
half, for easing me of the carriage.

Falstaff. Sir, I know not how I may deserve to be your
porter.

Ford. I will tell you, sir, if you will give me the hearing.

Falstaff. Speak, good Master Brook. I shall be glad to
be your servant.

Ford. Sir, I hear you are a scholar—I will be brief with
you—and you have been a man long known to me, though
I had never so good means, as desire, to make myself 170

acquainted with you....I shall discover a thing to you, wherein I must very much lay open mine own imperfection: but, good Sir John, as you have one eye upon my follies, as you hear them unfolded, turn another into the register of your own, that I may pass with a reproof the easier, sith you yourself know how easy it is to be such an offender.

Falstaff. Very well, sir. Proceed.

Ford. There is a gentlewoman in this town—her
180 husband's name is Ford.

Falstaff. Well, sir.

Ford. I have long loved her, and, I protest to you, bestowed much on her: followed her with a doting observance; engrossed opportunities to meet her; fee'd every slight occasion that could but niggardly give me sight of her; not only bought many presents to give her, but have given largely to many to know what she would have given: briefly, I have pursued her, as love hath pursued me, which hath been on the wing of all occasions...
190 but whatsoever I have merited—either in my mind or in my means—meed, I am sure, I have received none, unless experience be a jewel. That I have purchased at an infinite rate, and that hath taught me to say this—
"Love like a shadow flies when substance love pursues,
"Pursuing that that flies, and flying what pursues."

Falstaff. Have you received no promise of satisfaction at her hands?

Ford. Never.

Falstaff. Have you importuned her to such a purpose?
200 *Ford*. Never.

Falstaff. Of what quality was your love, then?

Ford. Like a fair house built upon another man's ground—so that I have lost my edifice by mistaking the place where I erected it.

Falstaff. To what purpose have you unfolded this to me?

Ford. When I have told you that, I have told you all...
Some say, that though she appear honest to me, yet in
other places she enlargeth her mirth so far that there is
shrewd construction made of her....Now, Sir John, here is
the heart of my purpose: you are a gentleman of excellent 210
breeding, admirable discourse, of great admittance,
authentic in your place and person, generally allowed for
your many war-like, court-like, and learned preparations.

Falstaff. O, sir!

Ford. Believe it, for you know it...[*he places the bag on
the table*] There is money. Spend it, spend it, spend more;
spend all I have, only give me so much of your time in
exchange of it, as to lay an amiable siege to the honesty
of this Ford's wife: use your art of wooing; win her to
consent to you: if any man may, you may as soon as any. 220

Falstaff. Would it apply well to the vehemency of your
affection, that I should win what you would enjoy?
Methinks you prescribe to yourself very preposterously.

Ford. O, understand my drift: she dwells so securely on
the excellency of her honour, that the folly of my soul
dares not present itself; she is too bright to be looked
against....Now, could I come to her with any detection
in my hand...my desires had instance and argument to
commend themselves. I could drive her then from the
ward of her purity, her reputation, her marriage-vow, 230
and a thousand other her defences, which now are too-too
strongly embattled against me: what say you to't, Sir John?

Falstaff [*weighing the bag in his hand*]. Master Brook,
I will first make bold with your money; next, give me
your hand; and last, as I am a gentleman, you shall, if
you will, enjoy Ford's wife.

Ford. O good sir!

Falstaff. I say you shall.

Ford. Want no money, Sir John, you shall want none.

240 *Falstaff.* Want no Mistress Ford, Master Brook, you shall want none: I shall be with her—I may tell you—by her own appointment. Even as you came in to me, her assistant, or go-between, parted from me: I say I shall be with her between ten and eleven; for at that time the jealous rascally knave, her husband, will be forth...Come you to me at night, you shall know how I speed.

Ford [*bowing*]. I am blest in your acquaintance...Do you know Ford, sir?

Falstaff. Hang him, poor cuckoldly knave! I know him

250 not: yet I wrong him to call him poor: they say the jealous wittolly knave hath masses of money, for the which his wife seems to me well-favoured: I will use her as the key of the cuckoldly rogue's coffer—and there's my harvest-home.

Ford. I would you knew Ford, sir, that you might avoid him, if you saw him.

Falstaff. Hang him, mechanical salt-butter rogue! I will stare him out of his wits: I will awe him with my cudgel: it shall hang like a meteor o'er the cuckold's horns...

260 Master Brook, thou shalt know, I will predominate over the peasant, and thou shalt lie with his wife....Come to me soon at night: Ford's a knave, and I will aggravate his style: thou, Master Brook, shalt know him for knave—and cuckold....Come to me soon at night.

[*he takes up the bag and goes*

Ford. What a damned Epicurean rascal is this! My heart is ready to crack with impatience...Who says this is improvident jealousy? my wife hath sent to him, the hour is fixed, the match is made...Would any man have thought this? See the hell of having a false woman: my

270 bed shall be abused, my coffers ransacked, my reputation gnawn at, and I shall not only receive this villainous

wrong, but stand under the adoption of abominable terms, and by him that does me this wrong...Terms, names! Amaimon sounds well; Lucifer, well; Barbason, well; yet they are devils' additions, the names of fiends: but Cuckold! Wittol!—Cuckold! the devil himself hath not such a name....Page is an ass, a secure ass; he will trust his wife, he will not be jealous: I will rather trust a Fleming with my butter, Parson Hugh the Welshman with my cheese, an Irishman with my aqua-vitæ bottle, 280 or a thief to walk my ambling gelding, than my wife with herself....Then she plots, then she ruminates, then she devises: and what they think in their hearts they may effect, they will break their hearts but they will effect.... God be praised for my jealousy...Eleven o'clock the hour. I will prevent this, detect my wife, be revenged on Falstaff, and laugh at Page....I will about it—better three hours too soon, than a minute too late....Fie, fie, fie! cuckold! cuckold! cuckold! *[he rushes from the room*

[2. 3.] *A field near Windsor*

*C*AIUS *and* RUGB*Y, walking to and fro*

Caius [*stops*]. Jack Rugby!

Rugby. Sir.

Caius. Vat is de clock, Jack?

Rugby. 'Tis past the hour, sir, that Sir Hugh promised to meet.

Caius. By gar, he has save his soul, dat he is no-come: he has pray his Pible well, dat he is no-come: by gar, Jack Rugby, he is dead already, if he be come.

Rugby. He is wise, sir: he knew your worship wou'd kill him if he came. 10

Caius. By gar, de herring is no dead, so as I vill kill him ...Take your rapier, Jack! I vill tell you how I vill kill him.

Rugby. Alas, sir, I cannot fence.

Caius. Villainy, take your rapier.   [*they begin to fence*

Rugby. Forbear...here's company.

HOST, SHALLOW, SLENDER, *and* PAGE *come up*

Host. Bless thee, bully doctor.

Shallow. Save you, Master Doctor Caius.

Page. Now, good master doctor!

Slender. Give you good-morrow, sir.

20   *Caius.* Vat be all you, one, two, tree, four, come for?

Host. To see thee fight, to see thee foin, to see thee traverse, to see thee here, to see thee there, to see thee pass thy punto, thy stock, thy reverse, thy distance, thy montánt...Is he dead, my Ethiopian? is he dead, my Francisco? ha, bully! What says my Æsculapius? my Galen? my heart of elder? Ha! is he dead, bully-stale? is he dead?

Caius. By gar, he is de Coward-Jack-Priest of de vorld: he is not show his face.

30   *Host.* Thou art a Castilian-King-Urinal! Hector of Greece, my boy!

Caius. I pray you, bear vitness that me have stay six or seven, two, tree hours for him, and he is no-come.

Shallow. He is the wiser man, master doctor! he is a curer of souls, and you a curer of bodies: if you should fight, you go against the hair of your professions: is it not true, Master Page?

Page. Master Shallow...you have yourself been a great fighter, though now a man of peace.

40   *Shallow.* Bodykins, Master Page, though I now be old, and of the peace...if I see a sword out, my finger itches to make one...Though we are justices, and doctors, and churchmen, Master Page, we have some salt of our youth in us—we are the sons of women, Master Page.

Page. 'Tis true, Master Shallow.

Shallow. It will be found so, Master Page...Master Doctor Caius, I am come to fetch you home...I am sworn of the peace: you have showed yourself a wise physician, and Sir Hugh hath shown himself a wise and patient churchman...You must go with me, master doctor. 50

Host. Pardon, guest-justice...a [word,] Mounseur †Mock-water.

Caius. Mock-vater? vat is dat?

Host. Mock-water, in our English tongue, is valour, bully.

Caius. By gar, then I have as much mock-vater as de Englishman...scurvy jack-dog priest! by gar, me vill cut his ears.

Host. He will clapper-claw thee tightly, bully. 60

Caius. Clapper-de-claw! vat is dat?

Host. That is, he will make thee amends.

Caius. By gar, me do look he shall clapper-de-claw me— for, by gar, me vill have it.

Host. And I will provoke him to't, or let him wag.

Caius. Me tank you for dat.

Host. And moreover, bully,—[*aside*] But first, master guest, and Master Page, and eke Cavaliero Slender, go you through the town to Frogmore.

(*Page.* Sir Hugh is there, is he? 70

(*Host.* He is there. See what humour he is in; and I will bring the doctor about by the fields: will it do well?

(*Shallow.* We will do it.

Page, Shallow, Slender. Adieu, good master doctor.

[*they depart*

Caius. By gar, me vill kill de priest, for he speak for a jack-an-ape to Anne Page.

Host. Let him die: [but, first,] sheathe thy impatience;

throw cold water on thy choler: go about the fields with
me through Frogmore. I will bring thee where Mistress
80 Anne Page is, at a farm-house a-feasting; and thou shalt
woo her...Cried-game, said I well?

Caius. By gar, me dank you vor dat: by gar, I love you;
and I shall procur-a you de good guest: de earl, de knight,
de lords, de gentlemen, my patients.

Host. For the which, I will be thy adversary toward
Anne Page: said I well?

Caius. By gar, 'tis good: vell said.

Host. Let us wag then.

Caius. Come at my heels, Jack Rugby.   [*they go off*

[3. 1.] *A meadow near Frogmore, with a field-path and
two stiles, one hard-by, the other at a distance: Sir* HUGH
EVANS, *in doublet and hose; a drawn sword in one hand
and an open book in the other.* SIMPLE *on the look-out
up a tree*

Evans [*calls*]. I pray you now, good Master Slender's
serving-man, and friend Simple by your name, which
way have you looked for Master Caius, that calls himself
doctor of physic?

Simple. Marry, sir, the †pittie-ward, the park-ward,
every way: old Windsor way, and every way but the town
way.

Evans. I most fehemently desire you, you will also look
that way.

10 *Simple.* I will, sir.

Evans. Pless my soul! how full of cholers I am, and
trempling of mind...I shall be glad, if he have deceived
me...how melancholies I am!—I will knog his urinals
about his knave's costard, when I have goot opportunities
for the 'ork...Pless my soul!   [*he sings*

To shallow rivers, to whose falls:
Melodious birds sing madrigals:
There will we make our peds of roses:
And a thousand fragrant posies....
      To shallow—   20
Mercy on me! I have a great dispositions to cry....
      Melodious birds sing madrigals—   [*he sings again*
When as I sat in Pabylon—
And a thousand vagram posies....
      To shallow, etc.—

Simple [*descending the tree*]. Yonder he is coming, this way, Sir Hugh.

Evans. He's welcome...[*sings*]To shallow rivers, to whose falls...Heaven prosper the right...What weapons is he?

Simple. No weapons, sir...[*points*] There comes my   30
master, Master Shallow, and another gentleman; from Frogmore, over the stile, this way.

Evans. Pray you, give me my gown—or else keep it in your arms.   [*Simple takes up the gown from the ground*

PAGE and SHALLOW come over the near stile, with SLENDER following. At the same time HOST, CAIUS and RUGBY are seen climbing the stile afar off

Shallow. How now, master parson! Good-morrow, good Sir Hugh...Keep a gamester from the dice, and a good student from his book, and it is wonderful.

Slender [*sighs*]. Ah, sweet Anne Page.

Page. Save you, good Sir Hugh.

Evans. Got-pless you from his mercy sake, all of you.   40

Shallow. What! the Sword and the Word! do you study them both, master parson?

Page. And youthful still, in your doublet and hose, this raw rheumatic day?

Evans. There is reasons and causes for it.

Page. We are come to you, to do a good office, master parson.

Evans. Fery well: what is it?

Page [*looking over Evans' shoulder*]. Yonder is a most
50 reverend gentleman; who belike, having received wrong
by some person, is at most odds with his own gravity and
patience that ever you saw.

Shallow. I have lived fourscore years and upward: I
never heard a man of his place, gravity, and learning, so
wide of his own respect.

Evans. What is he? [*Host, Caius and Rugby approach*
Page. I think you know him...[*Evans turns*] Master
Doctor Caius, the renowned French physician!

Evans. Got's will, and his passion of my heart! I had
60 as lief you would tell me of a mess of porridge.

Page. Why?

Evans. He has no more knowledge in Hibocrates and
Galen—[*raises his voice*] and he is a knave besides: a
cowardly knave as you would desires to be acquainted
withal. [*Caius runs forward with rapier and dagger drawn*
Page. I warrant you, he's the man should fight with
him.

Slender [*sighs*]. O, sweet Anne Page!

Shallow. It appears so, by his weapons...Keep them
70 asunder...Here comes Doctor Caius! [*he crosses his path*
Page [*steps in front of Evans*]. Nay, good master parson,
keep in your weapon.

Shallow. So do you, good master doctor.

Host. Disarm them, and let them question: let them
keep their limbs whole, and hack our English.

[*they are disarmed*
Caius. I pray you, let-a me speak a word with your ear;
Verefore vill you not meet-a me?

(*Evans*. Pray you, use your patience in good time.

Caius. By gar, you are de coward...de Jack-dog... John ape.   80

(*Evans.* Pray you, let us not be laughing-stogs to other men's humours: I desire you in friendship, and I will one way or other make you amends...

[*aloud*] I will knog your urinals about your knave's cogscomb, [for missing your meetings and appointments!]

Caius. Diable...Jack Rugby...mine host de Jarteer... have I not stay for him, to kill him? have I not, at de place I did appoint?

Evans. As I am a Christians-soul, now look you: this is the place appointed—I'll be judgement by mine host of   90 the Garter.

Host. Peace, I say, Gallia and Gaul, French and Welsh, soul-curer and body-curer.

Caius. Ay, dat is very good! excellent!

Host. Peace, I say; hear mine host of the Garter. Am I politic? am I subtle? am I a Machiavel? Shall I lose my doctor? no—he gives me the potions and the motions.... Shall I lose my parson? my priest? my Sir Hugh? no— he gives me the proverbs and the no-verbs....[Give me thy hand, terrestrial; so...] Give me thy hand, celestial;   100 so...[*joins their hands*] Boys of art, I have deceived you both: I have directed you to wrong places: your hearts are mighty, your skins are whole, and let burnt sack be the issue...[*to Page and Shallow*] Come, lay their swords to pawn...Follow me, lads of peace—follow, follow, follow.

[he mounts the stile

Shallow. Trust me, a mad host...Follow, gentlemen, follow.

Slender [*sighs*]. O, sweet Anne Page!

[Shallow, Page and Slender follow Host

Caius. Ha! do I perceive dat? have you mak-a de sot of us? ha, ha!   110

Evans. This is well! he has made us his vlouting-stog...
I desire you that we may be friends: and let us knog our
prains together to be revenge on this same scall, scurvy,
cogging companion, the host of the Garter.

Caius. By gar, with all my heart: he promise to bring
me where is Anne Page: by gar, he deceive me too.

Evans. Well, I will smite his noddles...Pray you, follow.

[they climb the stile

[3. 2.] *A street in Windsor, near the house of Master Ford*
*Mistress PAGE approaches with ROBIN strutting before
her; he pauses*

Mistress Page. Nay, keep your way, little gallant; you
were wont to be a follower, but now you are a leader...
Whether had you rather, lead mine eyes or eye your
master's heels?

Robin. I had rather, forsooth, go before you like a man
than follow him like a dwarf.

Mistress Page. O you are a flattering boy. Now, I see,
you'll be a courtier.

FORD comes up the street.

Ford. Well met, Mistress Page....Whither go you?

10 *Mistress Page.* Truly, sir, to see your wife. Is she at
home?

Ford. Ay—and as idle as she may hang together, for
want of company: I think, if your husbands were dead,
you two would marry.

Mistress Page. Be sure of that—two other husbands.

Ford. Where had you this pretty weathercock?

Mistress Page. I cannot tell what the dickens his name
is my husband had him of. What do you call your knight's
name, sirrah?

20 *Robin.* Sir John Falstaff.

Ford. Sir John Falstaff!

Mistress Page. He, he—I can never hit on's name; there is such a league between my good man and he! Is your wife at home, indeed?

Ford. Indeed she is.

Mistress Page [*curtsies*]. By your leave, sir. I am sick, till I see her.   [*she hurries on, with Robin before her*

  Ford. Has Page any brains? hath he any eyes? hath he any thinking? Sure, they sleep—he hath no use of them... Why, this boy will carry a letter twenty mile as easy—as 30 a cannon will shoot point blank twelve score! He pieces out his wife's inclination; he gives her folly motion and advantage: and now she's going to my wife, and Falstaff's boy with her...A man may hear this shower sing in the wind...and Falstaff's boy with her...good plots, they are laid, and our revolted wives share damnation together... Well, I will take him, then torture my wife, pluck the borrowed veil of modesty from the so-seeming Mistress Page, divulge Page himself for a secure and wilful Actæon—and to these violent proceedings all my neighbours shall cry aim.... 40 [*the town-clock strikes*] The clock gives me my cue, and my assurance bids me search—there I shall find Falstaff...I shall be rather praised for this than mocked; for it is as positive as the earth is firm that Falstaff is there...I will go.

Turning, he meets PAGE, SHALLOW, SLENDER, HOST, *Sir* HUGH EVANS, CAIUS, *and* RUGBY *coming up the street*

  All. Well met, Master Ford.

  Ford. Trust me, a good knot; I have good cheer at home, and I pray you all go with me.

  Shallow. I must excuse myself, Master Ford.

  Slender. And so must I, sir. We have appointed to dine with Mistress Anne, and I would not break with her for 50 more money than I'll speak of.

Shallow. We have lingered about a match between Anne
Page and my cousin Slender, and this day we shall have
our answer.

Slender. I hope I have your good will, father Page.

Page. You have, Master Slender. I stand wholly for
you—but my wife, master doctor, is for you altogether.

Caius. Ay, be-gar, and de maid is lov-a me: my nursh-a
Quickly tell me so mush.

60 *Host.* What say you to young Master Fenton? he capers,
he dances, he has eyes of youth…he writes verses, he
speaks holiday, he smells April and May. He will carry't,
he will carry't—'tis in his †buttons—he will carry't.

Page. Not by my consent, I promise you.…The gentleman is of no having—he kept company with the wild
Prince and Poins: he is of too high a region, he knows too
much…No, he shall not knit a knot in his fortunes with
the finger of my substance: if he take her, let him take
her simply: the wealth I have waits on my consent, and
70 my consent goes not that way.

Ford. I beseech you, heartily, some of you go home with
me to dinner: besides your cheer, you shall have sport—
I will show you a monster! Master doctor, you shall go—
so shall you, Master Page—and you, Sir Hugh.

Shallow. Well, fare you well: we shall have the freer
wooing at Master Page's.   [*he goes off with Slender*

Caius. Go home, John Rugby. I come anon.
                                    [*Rugby obeys*

Host. Farewell, my hearts. I will to my honest knight
Falstaff, and drink canary with him.   [*he follows Rugby*
80 (*Ford.* I think I shall drink in pipe-wine first with him—
I'll make him dance!

[*aloud*] Will you go, gentles?

Page, Caius, Evans. Have with you, to see this monster.
                                    [*they go with Ford*

[3. 3.] *The hall of Master Ford's house, hung with arras; stairs leading to a gallery; a large open hearth; three doors, one with windows right and left opening into the street*

Mistress FORD *and Mistress* PAGE, *bustling*

Mistress Ford [*calls*]. What, John! what, Robert!
Mistress Page. Quickly, quickly...is the buck-basket—
Mistress Ford. I warrant....What, Robin, I say!

Two servants enter carrying a large basket

Mistress Page [*impatient*]. Come, come, come!
Mistress Ford. Here, set it down.   [*they do so*
Mistress Page. Give your men the charge. We must be brief.
Mistress Ford. Marry, as I told you before, John and Robert, be ready here hard by in the brew-house, and when I suddenly call you, come forth, and—without any 10 pause or staggering—take this basket on your shoulders: that done, trudge with it in all haste, and carry it among the whitsters in Datchet-mead, and there empty it in the muddy ditch, close by the Thames side.
Mistress Page. You will do it?
Mistress Ford. I ha' told them over and over. They lack no direction....Be gone, and come when you are called.   [*the servants go out; Robin enters*
Mistress Page. Here comes little Robin.
Mistress Ford. How now, my eyas-musket! what news 20 with you?
Robin. My master, Sir John, is come in at your back-door, Mistress Ford, and requests your company.
Mistress Page. You little Jack-a-lent, have you been true to us?

Robin. Ay, I'll be sworn...My master knows not of your being here: and hath threatened to put me into ever-lasting liberty, if I tell you of it; for he swears he'll turn me away.

30 *Mistress Page.* Thou'rt a good boy: this secrecy of thine shall be a tailor to thee, and shall make thee a new doublet and hose....I'll go hide me.

Mistress Ford. Do so...Go tell thy master, I am alone... [*he goes*] Mistress Page, remember you your cue.

Mistress Page. I warrant thee. If I do not act it, hiss me.

Mistress Ford. Go to then: we'll use this unwholesome humidity, this gross watery pumpion; we'll teach him to know turtles from jays.

Mistress PAGE goes forth by one door, leaving it ajar; FALSTAFF enters by another

40 *Falstaff.* 'Have I caught my heavenly jewel?'
Why, now let me die, for I have lived long enough...This is the period of my ambition...O this blessed hour!

Mistress Ford. O sweet Sir John!   [*they embrace*

Falstaff. Mistress Ford, I cannot cog, I cannot prate, Mistress Ford. Now shall I sin in my wish; I would thy husband were dead. I'll speak it before the best lord, I would make thee my lady.

Mistress Ford. I your lady, Sir John! alas, I should be a pitiful lady.

50 *Falstaff.* Let the court of France show me such another: I see how thine eye would emulate the diamond: thou hast the right arched beauty of the brow that becomes the ship-tire, the tire-valiant, or any tire of Venetian admittance.

Mistress Ford. A plain kerchief, Sir John: my brows become nothing else—nor that well, neither.

Falstaff. Thou art a tyrant to say so: thou wouldst make an absolute courtier, and the firm fixture of thy foot would give an excellent motion to thy gait, in a semi-circled farthingale....I see what thou wert, if fortune thy 60 foe were not, nature thy friend...Come, thou canst not hide it.

Mistress Ford.   Believe me, there's no such thing in me.

Falstaff.   What made me love thee? let that persuade thee there's something extraordinary in thee...Come, I cannot cog and say thou art this and that, like a many of these lisping hawthorn-buds, that come like women in men's apparel, and smell like Bucklersbury in simple-time: I cannot—but I love thee, none but thee; and thou 70 deserv'st it.

Mistress Ford.   Do not betray me, sir. I fear you love Mistress Page.

Falstaff. Thou mightst as well say, I love to walk by the Counter-gate, which is as hateful to me as the reek of a lime-kiln.

Mistress Ford. Well, heaven knows how I love you—[*with meaning*] and you shall one day find it.

Falstaff.   Keep in that mind. I'll deserve it.

Mistress Ford.   Nay, I must tell you, so you do; [*with* 80 *meaning*] or else I could not be in that mind.

R<small>OBIN</small> enters, in haste

Robin. Mistress Ford, Mistress Ford! here's Mistress Page at the door, sweating, and blowing, and looking wildly, and would needs speak with you presently.

Falstaff. She shall not see me. I will ensconce me behind the arras.

Mistress Ford.   Pray you, do so—she's a very tattling woman....   [*Falstaff stands behind the arras*

Mistress PAGE comes from her hiding-place

What's the matter? how now!

90 *Mistress Page* [*seeming breathless*]. O Mistress Ford, what have you done? You're shamed, you're overthrown, you're undone for ever!

Mistress Ford. What's the matter, good Mistress Page?

Mistress Page. O well-a-day, Mistress Ford! having an honest man to your husband, to give him such cause of suspicion!

Mistress Ford. What cause of suspicion?

Mistress Page. What cause of suspicion! Out upon you! how am I mistook in you!

100 *Mistress Ford.* Why, alas, what's the matter?

Mistress Page. Your husband's coming hither, woman, with all the officers in Windsor, to search for a gentleman that he says is here now in the house—by your consent—to take an ill advantage of his absence...You are undone.

Mistress Ford. 'Tis not so, I hope.

Mistress Page. Pray heaven it be not so, that you have such a man here: but 'tis most certain your husband's coming, with half Windsor at his heels, to search for such

110 a one. I come before to tell you...If you know yourself clear, why I am glad of it: but if you have a friend here, convey, convey him out....Be not amazed, call all your senses to you, defend your reputation, or bid farewell to your good life for ever.

Mistress Ford. What shall I do? There is a gentleman, my dear friend: and I fear not mine own shame so much— as his peril....I had rather than a thousand pound, he were out of the house.

Mistress Page. For shame, never stand 'you had rather,'

120 and 'you had rather': your husband's here at hand!

Bethink you of some conveyance: in the house you cannot hide him....O, how have you deceived me! Look, here is a basket, if he be of any reasonable stature, he may creep in here—and throw foul linen upon him, as if it were going to bucking: or—it is whiting-time—send him by your two men to Datchet-mead.

Mistress Ford. He's too big to go in there: what shall I do?

FALSTAFF thrusting the arras aside, rushes towards the basket

Falstaff. Let me see't, let me see't, O let me see't...I'll in, I'll in...follow your friend's counsel—I'll in.   130
                         [he plucks out the linen
Mistress Page. What! Sir John Falstaff! [*in his ear*] Are these your letters, knight?

Falstaff [*climbing into the basket*]. I love thee, help me away...let me creep in here...I'll never—

Voices heard in the street without; he crouches; they cover him with foul linen

Mistress Page. Help to cover your master, boy! Call your men, Mistress Ford....You dissembling knight!

Mistress Ford [*calling*]. What, John, Robert, John!

ROBIN hastily thrusts the remainder of the linen into the basket and runs off; the servants enter swiftly

Go take up these clothes here, quickly...Where's the cowl-staff? look, how you drumble...[*they pass a pole* 140 *through the handles of the basket*] Carry them to the laundress in Datchet-mead...[*they hoist the basket, staggering*] quickly, come!

The door opens; FORD, PAGE, CAIUS, and
Sir HUGH EVANS enter from the street

Ford. Pray you, come near: if I suspect without cause,
why then make sport at me, then let me be your jest—
I deserve it...How now! [who goes here?] whither bear
you this?

Servants. To the laundress, forsooth.

Mistress Ford. Why, what have you to do whither they
150 bear it? You were best meddle with buck-washing.

Ford. Buck? I would I could wash myself of the buck!
Buck, buck, buck! Ay, buck: I warrant you, buck—and
of the season too it shall appear....[*the servants bear away
the basket*] Gentlemen, I have dreamed to-night. I'll tell
you my dream...Here, here, here be my keys. Ascend
my chambers, search, seek, find out: I'll warrant we'll
unkennel the fox....[*goes to the outer door*] Let me stop
this way first...[*locks it*] So, now †untapis!

Page. Good Master Ford, be contented: you wrong
160 yourself too much.

Ford. True, Master Page. Up, gentlemen--you shall see
sport anon...[*mounts the stairs*] Follow me, gentlemen.

                                                    [*they hesitate*

Evans. This is fery fantastical humours and jealousies.

Caius. By gar, 'tis no the fashion of France: it is not
jealous in France.

Page. Nay, follow him, gentlemen. See the issue of his
search.   [*they go up*

Mistress Page. Is there not a double excellency in this?

Mistress Ford. I know not which pleases me better, that
170 my husband is deceived, or Sir John.

Mistress Page. What a taking was he in, when your
husband asked who was in the basket!

Mistress Ford. I am half afraid he will have need of

washing: so throwing him into the water will do him a benefit.

Mistress Page. Hang him, dishonest rascal...I would all of the same strain were in the same distress.

Mistress Ford. I think my husband hath some special suspicion of Falstaff's being here; for I never saw him so gross in his jealousy till now.   180

Mistress Page. I will lay a plot to try that—and we will yet have more tricks with Falstaff: his dissolute disease will scarce obey this medicine.

Mistress Ford. Shall we send that foolish carrion, Mistress Quickly, to him, and excuse his throwing into the water, and give him another hope, to betray him to another punishment?

Mistress Page. We will do it: let him be sent for to-morrow, eight o'clock, to have amends.

The seekers return down the stairs

Ford. I cannot find him: may be the knave bragged 190
of that he could not compass.

(*Mistress Page.* Heard you that?

Mistress Ford. You use me well, Master Ford, do you?

Ford. Ay, I do so.

Mistress Ford. Heaven make you better than your thoughts.

Ford. Amen.

Mistress Page. You do yourself mighty wrong, Master Ford.

Ford. Ay, ay: I must bear it.   200

Evans. If there be any pody in the house, and in the chambers, and in the coffers, and in the presses...heaven forgive my sins at the day of judgement!

Caius. By gar, nor I too: there is no bodies.

Page. Fie, fie, Master Ford! are you not ashamed?

What spirit, what devil suggests this imagination? I
would not ha' your distemper in this kind, for the wealth
of Windsor Castle.

Ford. 'Tis my fault, Master Page—I suffer for it.

210 *Evans.* You suffer for a pad conscience: your wife is
as honest a 'omans, as I will desires among five thousand,
and five hundred too.

Caius. By gar, I see 'tis an honest woman.

Ford. Well, I promised you a dinner...Come, come,
walk in the Park. I pray you, pardon me: I will hereafter
make known to you why I have done this....Come, wife;
come, Mistress Page—I pray you pardon me....[*takes their
hands*] Pray heartily, pardon me.

        [*Mistress Ford and Mistress Page go to prepare dinner*

Page [*to the others*]. Let's go in, gentlemen—but, trust
220 me, we'll mock him...I do invite you to-morrow morning
to my house to breakfast: after, we'll a-birding together—
I have a fine hawk for the bush....Shall it be so?

Ford. Any thing.

Evans. If there is one, I shall make two in the company.

Caius. If there be one or two, I shall mak-a the turd.

Ford. Pray you go, Master Page.

            [*Ford and Page go forth to the Park*

Evans. I pray you now, remembrance to-morrow on
the lousy knave, mine host.

Caius. Dat is good, by gar—vit all my heart.

230 *Evans.* A lousy knave, to have his gibes and his mockeries.

            [*they follow Ford and Page*

[3. 4.]   *Before the house of Master Page*
          FENTON and ANNE seated, under the trees

Fenton. I see I cannot get thy father's love,
Therefore no more turn me to him, sweet Nan.

Anne. Alas, how then?

Fenton.   Why, thou must be thyself....
He doth object I am too great of birth,
And that, my state being galled with my expense,
I seek to heal it only by his wealth....
Besides these, other bars he lays before me—
My riots past, my wild societies—
And tells me 'tis a thing impossible
I should love thee but as a property...   10
    Anne. May be he tells you true.
    Fenton. No, heaven so speed me in my time to come!
Albeit I will confess thy father's wealth
Was the first motive that I wooed thee, Anne:
Yet, wooing thee, I found thee of more value
Than stamps in gold or sums in sealéd bags:
And 'tis the very riches of thyself
That now I aim at.
    Anne.   Gentle Master Fenton,
Yet seek my father's love—still seek it, sir.
If opportunity and humblest suit   20
Cannot attain it, why then hark you hither!

> *The house-door opens suddenly;* S H A L L O W *and*
> S L E N D E R *come forth with Mistress* Q U I C K L Y

Shallow. Break their talk, Mistress Quickly. My kinsman
shall speak for himself.   [*she draws near the lovers*
    Slender [*pale*]. I'll make a shaft or a bolt on't. 'Slid, 'tis
but venturing.
    Shallow. Be not dismayed.
    Slender. No, she shall not dismay me: I care not for
that—but that I am afeard.
    Quickly [*to Anne*]. Hark ye, Master Slender would
speak a word with you.   30
    Anne. I come to him....[*to Fenton*] This is my father's
    choice:

O, what a world of vile ill-favoured faults
Looks handsome in three hundred pounds a-year!
  Quickly [*steps between them*]. And how does good Master
Fenton? Pray you, a word with you. [*Anne moves away*
  Shallow. She's coming; to her, coz...O boy, thou hadst
a father!
  Slender. I had a father, Mistress Anne. My uncle can
tell you good jests of him: pray you, uncle, tell Mistress
40 Anne the jest, how my father stole two geese out of a
pen, good uncle.
  Shallow. Mistress Anne, my cousin loves you.
  Slender. Ay, that I do—as well as I love any woman in
Gloucestershire.
  Shallow. He will maintain you like a gentlewoman.
  Slender. Ay, that I will, come cut and long-tail—under
the degree of a squire.
  Shallow. He will make you a hundred and fifty pounds
jointure.
50 *Anne*. Good Master Shallow, let him woo for himself.
  Shallow. Marry, I thank you for it: I thank you for that
good comfort...She calls you, coz. I'll leave you.
                                         [*he stands aside*

  Anne. Now, Master Slender.
  Slender [*plucking at his beard*]. Now, good Mistress
Anne.
  Anne. What is your will?
  Slender. My will! od's heartlings, that's a pretty jest,
indeed. I ne'er made my will yet, I thank heaven! I am
not such a sickly creature, I give heaven praise.
60 *Anne*. I mean, Master Slender, what would you with
me?
  Slender [*casting down his eyes*]. Truly, for mine own part,
I would little or nothing with you...Your father and my
uncle hath made motions: if it be my luck, so; if not,

happy man be his dole! They can tell you how things
go, better than I can: you may ask your father; here he
comes.

    PAGE and Mistress PAGE come up, returning
            from Master Ford's house

Page. Now, Master Slender; love him, daughter Anne....
Why, how now! what does Master Fenton here?
You wrong me, sir, thus still to haunt my house....   70
I told you, sir, my daughter is disposed of.
  Fenton. Nay, Master Page, be not impatient.
  Mistress Page. Good Master Fenton, come not to
    my child.
  Page. She is no match for you.
  Fenton. Sir, will you hear me?
  Page.   No, good Master Fenton....
Come, Master Shallow; come, son Slender, in...
Knowing my mind, you wrong me, Master Fenton.
              [*Page, Shallow and Slender enter the house*
  (*Quickly.* Speak to Mistress Page.
  Fenton. Good Mistress Page, for that I love your
    daughter
In such a righteous fashion as I do,   80
Perforce, against all checks, rebukes and manners,
I must advance the colours of my love,
And not retire....Let me have your good will.
  Anne. Good mother, do not marry me to yond fool.
  Mistress Page. I mean it not. I seek you a better
    husband.
  Quickly. That's my master, master doctor.
  Anne. Alas, I had rather be set quick i'th'earth,
And bowled to death with turnips.
  Mistress Page. Come, trouble not yourself good Master
    Fenton,
I will not be your friend nor enemy: 90

M.W.W.—7

My daughter will I question how she loves you,
And as I find her, so am I affected:
Till then, farewell, sir. She must needs go in—
Her father will be angry.

Mistress Page goes in; Anne follows, turning at the door

Fenton. Farewell, gentle mistress: farewell, Nan.

[the door closes

Quickly. This is my doing now: 'Nay,' said I, 'will you cast away your child on a fool, and a physician? Look on Master Fenton.' This is my doing.

Fenton. I thank thee; and I pray thee, once to-night
100 Give my sweet Nan this ring...There's for thy pains.

He thrusts money in her hand and departs

Quickly. Now heaven send thee good fortune! A kind heart he hath: a woman would run through fire and water for such a kind heart....[*pockets the coin*] But yet, I would my master had Mistress Anne; or I would Master Slender had her; or, in sooth, I would Master Fenton had her: I will do what I can for them all three— for so I have promised, and I'll be as good as my word, but speciously for Master Fenton....Well, I must of another errand to Sir John Falstaff from my two mistresses:
110 what a beast am I to slack it!   [*she hurries away*

[3. 5.] *The room in the Garter Inn: early morning*
FALSTAFF descends from his chamber

Falstaff [*calling*]. Bardolph, I say!

Bardolph [*runs in*]. Here, sir.

Falstaff. Go fetch me a quart of sack—put a toast in't....[*Bardolph goes; Falstaff sits*] Have I lived to be carried in a basket, like a barrow of butcher's offal, and to be thrown in the Thames? Well, if I be served such another trick, I'll have my brains ta'en out, and buttered,

and give them to a dog for a new-year's gift....The
rogues slighted me into the river with as little remorse
as they would have drowned a blind bitch's puppies, 10
fifteen i'th' litter: and you may know by my size, that
I have a kind of alacrity in sinking; if the bottom were
as deep as hell, I should down....I had been drowned, but
that the shore was shelvy and shallow...a death that I
abhor; for the water swells a man; and what a thing should
I have been, when I had been swelled! I should have
been a mountain of mummy.

BARDOLPH *returns with two cups of sack*

Bardolph. Here's Mistress Quickly, sir, to speak with
you.   [*he sets the cups down*
Falstaff [*takes one*]. Come, let me pour in some sack to 20
the Thames water; for my belly's as cold as if I had
swallowed snowballs for pills to cool the reins....[*he drains
the cup*] Call her in.
Bardolph [*opening the door*]. Come in, woman.

Mistress QUICKLY *enters and curtsies*

Quickly. By your leave...I cry you mercy! Give your
worship good-morrow.
Falstaff [*empties the second cup*]. Take away these
chalices...Go brew me a pottle of sack finely.
Bardolph [*takes up the empty cups*]. With eggs, sir?
Falstaff. Simple of itself; I'll no pullet-sperm in my 30
brewage....[*Bardolph leaves*] How now!
Quickly. Marry, sir, I come to your worship from
Mistress Ford.
Falstaff. Mistress Ford! I have had ford enough: I was
thrown into the ford; I have my belly full of ford.
Quickly. Alas the day! good heart, that was not her
fault: she does so take on with her men; they mistook
their erection.

Falstaff. So did I mine, to build upon a foolish woman's
40 promise.

Quickly. Well, she laments, sir, for it, that it would
yearn your heart to see it...Her husband goes this
morning a-birding; she desires you once more to come
to her, between eight and nine: I must carry her word
quickly. She'll make you amends, I warrant you.

Falstaff. Well, I will visit her. Tell her so; and bid her
think what a man is: let her consider his frailty, and then
judge of my merit.

Quickly. I will tell her.

50 *Falstaff*. Do so....Between nine and ten, sayst thou?

Quickly. Eight and nine, sir.

Falstaff. Well, be gone: I will not miss her.

Quickly. Peace be with you, sir!   [*she goes*

Falstaff. I marvel I hear not of Master Brook; he sent
me word to stay within: I like his money well....O, here
he comes.

FORD *enters, disguised as* BROOK

Ford. Bless you, sir!

Falstaff. Now, Master Brook—you come to know what
hath passed between me and Ford's wife?

60 *Ford*. That, indeed, Sir John, is my business.

Falstaff. Master Brook, I will not lie to you. I was at
her house the hour she appointed me—

Ford. And sped you, sir?

Falstaff. Very ill-favouredly, Master Brook.

Ford. How so, sir? Did she change her determination?

Falstaff. No, Master Brook—but the peaking cornuto
her husband, Master Brook, dwelling in a continual 'larum
of jealousy, comes me in the instant of our encounter,
after we had embraced, kissed, protested, and, as it were,
70 spoke the prologue of our comedy; and at his heels a

rabble of his companions, thither provoked and instigated
by his distemper, and, forsooth, to search his house for
his wife's love.

Ford. What! while you were there?

Falstaff. While I was there.

Ford. And did he search for you, and could not find
you?

Falstaff. You shall hear....As good luck would have it,
comes in one Mistress Page, gives intelligence of Ford's
approach...and, in her invention and Ford's wife's dis- 80
traction, they conveyed me into a buck-basket.

Ford. A buck-basket!

Falstaff. [By the Lord,] a buck-basket: rammed me in
with foul shirts and smocks, socks, foul stockings, greasy
napkins—that, Master Brook, there was the rankest compound of villainous smell, that ever offended nostril.

Ford. And how long lay you there?

Falstaff. Nay, you shall hear, Master Brook, what I have
suffered to bring this woman to evil for your good...Being
thus crammed in the basket, a couple of Ford's knaves, 90
his hinds, were called forth by their mistress, to carry me
in the name of foul clothes to Datchet-lane: they took
me on their shoulders; met the jealous knave their master
in the door; who asked them once or twice what they had
in their basket! I quaked for fear, lest the lunatic knave
would have searched it; but fate, ordaining he should be
a cuckold, held his hand...Well, on went he for a search,
and away went I for foul clothes: but mark the sequel,
Master Brook. I suffered the pangs of three several deaths:
first, an intolerable fright, to be detected with a jealous 100
rotten bell-wether; next, to be compassed, like a good
bilbo, **in** the circumference of a peck, hilt to point, heel
to head....and then, to be stopped in, like a strong distillation, with stinking clothes that fretted in their own

grease...think of that—a man of my kidney; think of that—that am as subject to heat, as butter; a man of continual dissolution and thaw; it was a miracle to 'scape suffocation....And in the height of this bath, when I was more than half stewed in grease, like a Dutch dish, to be

110 thrown into the Thames, and cooled, glowing-hot (in that surge!) like a horse-shoe; think of that—hissing hot; think of that, Master Brook!

Ford. In good sadness, sir, I am sorry that for my sake you have suffered all this....My suit then is desperate: you'll undertake her no more?

Falstaff. Master Brook...I will be thrown into Etna, as I have been into Thames, ere I will leave her thus...Her husband is this morning gone a-birding: I have received from her another embassy of meeting: 'twixt eight and

120 nine is the hour, Master Brook.

Ford. 'Tis past eight already, sir.

Falstaff. Is it? I will then address me to my appointment...Come to me at your convenient leisure, and you shall know how I speed: and the conclusion shall be crowned with your enjoying her...Adieu...You shall have her, Master Brook. Master Brook, you shall cuckold Ford.

[*he goes out*

Ford. Hum...ha! is this a vision? is this a dream? do I sleep? Master Ford awake, awake Master Ford! there's a hole made in your best coat, Master Ford...This 'tis to

130 be married; this 'tis to have linen and buck-baskets... Well, I will proclaim myself what I am: I will now take the lecher: he is at my house: he cannot 'scape me: 'tis impossible he should: he cannot creep into a halfpenny purse, nor into a pepper-box...But, lest the devil that guides him should aid him, I will search impossible places ...Though what I am I cannot avoid, yet to be what I would not shall not make me tame: if I have horns to

make one mad, let the proverb go with me—I'll be horn-
mad.   *[he rushes out*

[4. 1.]   *The street before the house of Master Page*
     Mistress PAGE comes forth with Mistress QUICKLY,
                     and WILLIAM

Mistress Page. Is he at Master Ford's already, think'st
thou?

Quickly. Sure, he is by this; or will be presently; but
truly he is very courageous mad, about his throwing into
the water....Mistress Ford desires you to come suddenly.

Mistress Page. I'll be with her by and by: I'll but bring
my young man here to school...Look where his master
comes; 'tis a playing-day, I see...

         Sir HUGH EVANS approaches

How now, Sir Hugh! no school to-day?

Evans. No: Master Slender is let the boys leave to play. 10

Quickly. Blessing of his heart!

Mistress Page. Sir Hugh, my husband says my son
profits nothing in the world at his book: I pray you, ask
him some questions in his accidence.

Evans. Come hither, William; hold up your head;
come.

Mistress Page. Come on, sirrah; hold up your head;
answer your master, be not afraid.

Evans. William, how many numbers is in nouns?

William. Two.   20

Quickly. Truly, I thought there had been one number
more; because they say, 'Od's nouns.'

Evans. Peace your tattlings! What is 'fair,' William?

William. Pulcher.

Quickly. Polecats! there are fairer things than polecats,
sure.

Evans. You are a very simplicity 'oman: I pray you, peace....What is 'lapis,' William?

William. A stone.

30 *Evans.* And what is 'a stone,' William?

William. A pebble.

Evans. No; it is 'lapis': I pray you remember in your prain.

William. Lapis.

Evans. That is a good William...What is he, William, that does lend articles?

William. Articles are borrowed of the pronoun; and be thus declined, Singulariter, nominativo, hic, hæc, hoc.

Evans. Nominativo, hig, hag, hog: pray you, mark: genitivo, hujus...Well: what is your accusative case?

40 *William.* Accusativo, hinc.

Evans. I pray you, have your remembrance, child—accusativo, hung, hang, hog.

Quickly. 'Hang-hog' is Latin for bacon, I warrant you.

Evans. Leave your prabbles, 'oman....What is the focative case, William?

William [scratches his head]. O! vocativo—O.

Evans. Remember, William—focative is caret.

Quickly. And that's a good root.

Evans. 'Oman, forbear.

50 *Mistress Page.* Peace.

Evans. What is your genitive case plural, William?

William. Genitive case?

Evans. Ay.

William. Genitive—horum, harum, horum.

Quickly. Vengeance of Jenny's case! fie on her! never name her, child, if she be a whore.

Evans. For shame, 'oman.

Quickly. You do ill to teach the child such words: he teaches him to hick and to hack—which they'll do fast

60 enough of themselves, and to call 'horum'; fie upon you!

Evans. 'Oman, art thou lunatics? hast thou no under-
standings for thy cases, and the numbers of the genders?
Thou art as foolish Christian creatures as I would desires.

Mistress Page [*to Mistress Quickly*]. Prithee hold thy
peace.

Evans. Show me now, William, some declensions of
your pronouns.

William. Forsooth, I have forgot.

Evans. It is qui, quæ, quod; if you forget your qui's,
your quæ's, and your quod's, you must be preeches... 70
Go your ways and play, go.

Mistress Page. He is a better scholar than I thought he
was.

Evans. He is a good sprag memory...Farewell, Mistress
Page.   [*he pursues his way*

Mistress Page. Adieu, good Sir Hugh...Get you home,
boy. Come, we stay too long.

[*she goes off with Mistress Quickly*

[4. 2.]   *The hall in Master Ford's house; the*
buck-basket in a corner

FALSTAFF and Mistress FORD, seated

Falstaff. Mistress Ford, your sorrow hath eaten up my
sufferance; I see you are obsequious in your love, and
I profess requital to a hair's breadth, not only, Mistress
Ford, in the simple office of love, but in all the accoutrement, complement, and ceremony of it...But are you
sure of your husband now?

Mistress Ford. He's a-birding, sweet Sir John.

Mistress Page [*calling without*]. What ho, gossip Ford!
what ho!

Mistress Ford [*opening a door*]. Step into th' chamber, 10
Sir John.   [*Falstaff goes forth, leaving the door ajar*

Mistress PAGE enters

Mistress Page. How now, sweetheart! who's at home besides yourself?

Mistress Ford. Why, none but mine own people.

Mistress Page. Indeed?

Mistress Ford. No, certainly...[*whispers*] Speak louder.

Mistress Page. Truly, I am so glad you have nobody here.

Mistress Ford. Why?

Mistress Page. Why, woman, your husband is in his old
20 †lunes again: he so takes on yonder with my husband; so rails against all married mankind; so curses all Eve's daughters, of what complexion soever; and so buffets himself on the forehead, crying, 'Peer out, peer out!' that any madness I ever yet beheld seemed but tameness, civility, and patience, to this his distemper he is in now... I am glad the fat knight is not here.

Mistress Ford. Why, does he talk of him?

Mistress Page. Of none but him—and swears he was carried out the last time he searched for him in a basket;
30 protests to my husband he is now here; and hath drawn him and the rest of their company from their sport, to make another experiment of his suspicion...But I am glad the knight is not here; now he shall see his own foolery.

Mistress Ford. How near is he, Mistress Page?

Mistress Page. Hard by, at street end; he will be here anon.

Mistress Ford. I am undone!—the knight is here.

Mistress Page. Why, then you are utterly shamed, and
40 he's but a dead man....What a woman are you! Away with him, away with him: better shame than murder!

FALSTAFF peers forth from the chamber

Mistress Ford. Which way should he go? how should I bestow him? Shall I put him into the basket again?

Falstaff [*rushes forward*]. No, I'll come no more i'th' basket...May I not go out, ere he come?

Mistress Page. Alas: three of Master Ford's brothers watch the door with pistols, that none shall issue out: otherwise you might slip away ere he came...But what make you here?

Falstaff. What shall I do?—I'll creep up into the 50 chimney.

†*Mistress Page.* There they always use to discharge their birding-pieces...Creep into the kiln-hole.

Falstaff. Where is it?

Mistress Ford. He will seek there on my word...Neither press, coffer, chest, trunk, well, vault, but he hath an abstract for the remembrance of such places, and goes to them by his note...There is no hiding you in the house.

Falstaff [*at bay*]. I'll go out then.

†*Mistress Page.* If you go out in your own semblance, 60 you die, Sir John—unless you go out disguised.

Mistress Ford. How might we disguise him?

Mistress Page. Alas the day, I know not. There is no woman's gown big enough for him; otherwise, he might put on a hat, a muffler, and a kerchief, and so escape.

Falstaff. Good hearts, devise something: any extremity, rather than a mischief.

Mistress Ford. My maid's aunt, the fat woman of Brainford, has a gown above. 70

Mistress Page. On my word, it will serve him; she's as big as he is: and there's her thrummed hat, and her muffler too...Run up, Sir John.

Mistress Ford. Go, go, sweet Sir John...Mistress Page and I will look some linen for your head.

Mistress Page. Quick, quick! we'll come dress you straight: put on the gown the while.

> [*Falstaff posts up the stairs*

Mistress Ford. I would my husband would meet him in this shape: he cannot abide the old woman of Brain-
80 ford; he swears she's a witch, forbade her my house, and hath threatened to beat her.

Mistress Page. Heaven guide him to thy husband's cudgel: and the devil guide his cudgel afterwards!

Mistress Ford. But is my husband coming?

Mistress Page. Ay, in good sadness, is he—and talks of the basket too, howsoever he hath had intelligence.

Mistress Ford. We'll try that; for I'll appoint my men to carry the basket again, to meet him at the door with it, as they did last time.

90 *Mistress Page.* Nay, but he'll be here presently: let's go dress him like the witch of Brainford.

Mistress Ford. I'll first direct my men what they shall do with the basket...Go up, I'll bring linen for him straight.

Mistress Page. Hang him, dishonest varlet! we cannot misuse him enough...

> [*Mistress Ford goes out; Mistress Page mounts the stairs*
> We'll leave a proof, by that which we will do,
> Wives may be merry, and yet honest too:
> We do not act that often jest and laugh—
100 'Tis old but true, 'Still swine eats all the draff.'

Mistress FORD *returns with the two servants*

Mistress Ford. Go, sirs, take the basket again on your shoulders: your master is hard at door: if he bid you set it down, obey him...quickly, dispatch.

> [*she takes linen from a cupboard and goes upstairs*

First Servant. Come, come, take it up.

Second Servant. Pray heaven it be not full of knight again.

First Servant. I hope not. I had as lief bear so much lead.   [*they lift the basket*

The door opens; FORD, PAGE, SHALLOW, CAIUS, *and Sir* HUGH EVANS *enter from the street*

Ford. Ay, but if it prove true, Master Page, have you any way then to unfool me again? [*the basket catches* 110 *his eye*]....Set down the basket, villain...Somebody call my wife...Youth in a basket...O, you pandarly rascals! there's a knot...a ging, a pack, a conspiracy against me...Now shall the devil be shamed [*chokes*]....What! wife, I say...Come, come forth...Behold what honest clothes you send forth to bleaching!

Page. Why, this passes, Master Ford! you are not to go loose any longer—you must be pinioned.

Evans. Why, this is lunatics! this is mad, as a mad dog!   120

Shallow. Indeed, Master Ford, this is not well, indeed.

Ford. So say I too, sir. [*Mistress Ford appears in the gallery*] Come hither, Mistress Ford! [*pointing, as she descends*] Mistress Ford, the honest woman, the modest wife, the virtuous creature, that hath the jealous fool to her husband...[*she confronts him*] I suspect without cause, mistress, do I?

Mistress Ford [*calm*]. Heaven be my witness you do, if you suspect me in any dishonesty.

Ford. Well said, brazen-face, hold it out...Come forth, 130 sirrah.   [*plucking forth the clothes in a fury*

Page. This passes!

Mistress Ford. Are you not ashamed? let the clothes alone.

Ford. I shall find you anon.

Evans. 'Tis unreasonable! Will you take up your wife's clothes? [*to the others*] Come, away!

Ford [*to the servants*]. Empty the basket, I say.

Mistress Ford. Why, man, why?

140 *Ford.* Master Page, as I am a man, there was one conveyed out of my house yesterday in this basket: why may not he be there again? In my house I am sure he is: my intelligence is true, my jealousy is reasonable, pluck me out all the linen!   [*Page assists him*

Mistress Ford. If you find a man there, he shall die a flea's death.

Page. Here's no man.   [*he overturns the empty basket*

Shallow. By my fidelity, this is not well, Master Ford: this wrongs you.

150 *Evans.* Master Ford, you must pray, and not follow the imaginations of your own heart: this is jealousies.

Ford. Well, he's not here I seek for.

Page. No, nor nowhere else but in your brain.

Ford. Help to search my house this one time: if I find not what I seek, show no colour for my extremity...let me for ever be your table-sport...let them say of me, 'As jealous as Ford, that searched a hollow walnut for his wife's leman'....Satisfy me once more, once more search with me.

160 *Mistress Ford.* What ho, Mistress Page! come you and the old woman down: my husband will come into the chamber.

Ford. Old woman! What old woman's that?

Mistress Ford. Why, it is my maid's aunt of Brainford.

Ford. A witch, a quean, an old cozening quean! Have I not forbid her my house? She comes of errands, does she? We are simple men, we do not know what's brought to pass under the profession of fortune-telling....She works

by charms, by spells, by th' figure, and such daubery as 170
this is, beyond our element: we know nothing....[*he takes
down his cudgel from the wall*] Come down, you witch, you
hag you, come down, I say.

Mistress Ford. Nay, good, sweet husband—good gentlemen, let him not strike the old woman.

F A L S T A F F *descends in women's clothes, led by Mistress*
P A G E; *he hesitates near the foot of the stairs*

Mistress Page. Come, Mother Prat, come, give me
your hand.

Ford. I'll prat her...[*Falstaff runs; Ford cudgels*] Out of
my door, you witch, you rag, you baggage, you polecat,
you ronyon! out! out! I'll conjure you, I'll fortune-tell 180
you.   [*Falstaff escapes into the street*

Mistress Page. Are you not ashamed? I think, you have
killed the poor woman.

Mistress Ford. Nay, he will do it. 'Tis a goodly credit
for you.

Ford. Hang her, witch!   [*he mounts the stairs*

Evans. By yea and no, I think the 'oman is a witch
indeed: I like not when a 'oman has a great peard; I spy
a great peard under his muffler.

Ford [*from the gallery*]. Will you follow, gentlemen? I 190
beseech you, follow: see but the issue of my jealousy: if
I cry out thus upon no trail, never trust me when I open
again.

Page. Let's obey his humour a little further...Come,
gentlemen.   [*they follow*

Mistress Page. Trust me, he beat him most pitifully.

Mistress Ford. Nay, by th' mass, that he did not: he
beat him most unpitifully methought.

Mistress Page. I'll have the cudgel hallowed and hung
o'er the altar—it hath done meritorious service. 200

Mistress Ford. What think you? May we, with the warrant of womanhood and the witness of a good conscience, pursue him with any further revenge?

Mistress Page. The spirit of wantonness is, sure, scared out of him. If the devil have him not in fee-simple, with fine and recovery, he will never, I think, in the way of waste, attempt us again.

Mistress Ford. Shall we tell our husbands how we have served him?

210 *Mistress Page.* Yes, by all means; if it be but to scrape the figures out of your husband's brains...If they can find in their hearts the poor unvirtuous fat knight shall be any further afflicted, we two will still be the ministers.

Mistress Ford. I'll warrant they'll have him publicly shamed—and methinks there would be no period to the jest, should he not be publicly shamed.

Mistress Page. Come, to the forge with it! then shape it: I would not have things cool.

[*they go up together, talking*

[4. 3.]   *The room in the Garter Inn*
HOST and BARDOLPH enter

Bardolph. Sir, the Germans desire to have three of your horses: the duke himself will be to-morrow at court, and they are going to meet him.

Host. What duke should that be comes so secretly? I hear not of him in the court...Let me speak with the gentlemen—they speak English?

Bardolph. Ay, sir; I'll call them to you.

Host. They shall have my horses, but I'll make them pay: I'll sauce them. They have had my house a week at
10 command; I have turned away my other guests. They must come off. I'll sauce them, come.   [*they go out*

[4. 4.]   *The hall in Master Ford's house*

PAGE, FORD, *Mistress* PAGE, *Mistress* FORD, *and*
Sir HUGH EVANS, *holding lively conversation*

Evans. 'Tis one of the pest discretions of a 'oman as
ever I did look upon.

Page. And did he send you both these letters at an
instant?

Mistress Page. Within a quarter of an hour.

Ford [*kneeling*]. Pardon me, wife. Henceforth do what
        thou wilt:
I rather will suspect the sun with cold
Than thee with wantonness: now doth thy honour stand,
In him that was of late an heretic,
As firm as faith.

Page.   'Tis well, 'tis well—no more: 10
Be not as éxtreme in submission,
As in offence.
But let our plot go forward: let our wives
Yet once again, to make us public sport,
Appoint a meeting with this old fat fellow,
Where we may take him, and disgrace him for it.

Ford. There is no better way than that they spoke of.

Page. How? to send him word they'll meet him in the
Park at midnight? fie, fie! he'll never come.

Evans. You say he has been thrown in the rivers, and   20
has been grievously peaten, as an old 'oman: methinks
there should be terrors in him, that he should not
come: methinks his flesh is punished, he shall have no
desires.

Page. So think I too.

Mistress Ford. Devise but how you'll use him, when
        he comes,
And let us two devise to bring him thither.

Mistress Page. There is an old tale goes, that Herne
    the hunter,
Sometime a keeper here in Windsor forest,
30 Doth all the winter-time, at still midnight,
Walk round about an oak, with great ragg'd horns---
And there he blasts the tree, and takes the cattle,
And makes milch-kine yield blood, and shakes a chain
In a most hideous and dreadful manner....
You have heard of such a spirit, and well you know
The superstitious idle-headed eld
Received, and did deliver to our age,
This tale of Herne the hunter for a truth.
  Page. Why, yet there want not many that do fear
40 In deep of night to walk by this Herne's oak:
But what of this?
  Mistress Ford.   Marry, this is our device---
That Falstaff at that oak shall meet with us,
[Disguised like Herne, with huge horns on his head.]
  Page. Well, let it not be doubted but he'll come,
And in this shape. When you have brought him thither,
What shall be done with him? what is your plot?
  Mistress Page. That likewise have we thought upon,
    and thus:
Nan Page my daughter and my little son
And three or four more of their growth we'll dress
50 Like urchins, ouphs, and fairies, green and white,
With rounds of waxen tapers on their heads,
And rattles in their hands; upon a sudden,
As Falstaff, she, and I, are newly met,
Let them from forth a saw-pit rush at once
With some diffuséd song: upon their sight,
We two in great amazedness will fly:
Then let them all encircle him about,
And, fairy-like, to pinch the unclean knight;

And ask him why, that hour of fairy revel,
In their so sacred paths he dares to tread   60
In shape profane.
Mistress Ford.   And till he tell the truth,
Let the supposéd fairies pinch him sound,
And burn him with their tapers.
Mistress Page.   The truth being known,
We'll all present ourselves; dis-horn the spirit,
And mock him home to Windsor.
Ford.   The children must
Be practised well to this, or they'll ne'er do't.
Evans. I will teach the children their behaviours: and
I will be like a jack-an-apes also, to burn the knight with
my taber.
Ford. That will be excellent. I'll go buy them vizards. 70
Mistress Page. My Nan shall be the queen of all
       the fairies,
Finely attiréd in a robe of white.
Page. That silk will I go buy--[*aside*] and in that time
Shall Master Slender steal my Nan away,
And marry her at Eton...Go, send to Falstaff straight.
Ford [*to Page*]. Nay, I'll to him again in name of Brook:
He'll tell me all his purpose: sure, he'll come.
Mistress Page. Fear not you that...Go, get us properties,
And tricking for our fairies.
Evans. Let us about it: it is admirable pleasures and 80
fery honest knaveries.   [*Page, Ford, and Evans depart*
Mistress Page. Go, Mistress Ford,
Send Quickly to Sir John, to know his mind...
                              [*Mistress Ford goes*
I'll to the doctor—he hath my good will,
And none but he, to marry with Nan Page...
That Slender, though well landed, is an idiot;
And he my husband best of all affects:

The doctor is well moneyed, and his friends
Potent at court: he, none but he, shall have her,
90 Though twenty thousand worthier come to crave her.

[*she goes*

[4. 5.]   *The room in the Garter Inn*
        SIMPLE stands waiting; HOST enters in haste

Host. What wouldst thou have, boor? what, thick-skin?
speak, breathe, discuss; brief, short, quick, snap.

Simple. Marry, sir, I come to speak with Sir John
Falstaff from Master Slender.

Host [*points to the gallery*]. There's his chamber, his
house, his castle, his standing-bed, and truckle-bed; 'tis
painted about with the story of the Prodigal, fresh and
new: go, knock and call: he'll speak like an Anthropophaginian unto thee: knock, I say.

10 *Simple.* There's an old woman, a fat woman, gone up
into his chamber: I'll be so bold as stay, sir, till she come
down: I come to speak with her, indeed.

Host. Ha! a fat woman! the knight may be robbed:
I'll call....Bully knight! bully Sir John! speak from thy
lungs military: art thou there? it is thine host, thine
Ephesian, calls.

Falstaff [*opens the door of his chamber*]. How now, mine
host?

Host. Here's a Bohemian-Tartar tarries the coming
20 down of thy fat woman...Let her descend, bully, let her
descend: my chambers are honourable: fie! privacy? fie!

        FALSTAFF descends

Falstaff. There was, mine host, an old fat woman even
now with me—but she's gone.

Simple. Pray you, sir, was't not the wise woman of
Brainford?

Falstaff. Ay, marry, was it, mussel-shell—what would you with her?

Simple. My master, sir, Master Slender, sent to her, seeing her go thorough the streets, to know, sir, whether one Nym, sir, that beguiled him of a chain, had the chain, or no. 30

Falstaff. I spake with the old woman about it.

Simple. And what says she, I pray, sir?

Falstaff. Marry, she says that the very same man that beguiled Master Slender of his chain cozened him of it.

Simple. I would I could have spoken with the woman herself. I had other things to have spoken with her too, from him.

Falstaff. What are they? let us know.

Host. Ay...come...quick!

Simple. I may not conceal them, sir. 40

Host [*threatening him*]. Conceal them, or thou diest.

Simple. Why, sir, they were nothing but about Mistress Anne Page—to know if it were my master's fortune to have her, or no.

Falstaff. 'Tis, 'tis his fortune.

Simple. What, sir?

Falstaff. To have her, or no...Go; say the woman told me so.

Simple. May I be so bold to say so, sir?

Falstaff. Ay, Sir †Tyke; who more bold? 50

Simple. I thank your worship: I shall make my master glad with these tidings.　　　　　[*he goes out*

Host. Thou art clerkly! thou art clerkly, Sir John. Was there a wise woman with thee?

Falstaff. Ay, that there was, mine host—one that hath taught me more wit than ever I learned before in my life: and I paid nothing for it neither, but was paid for my learning.

BARDOLPH enters, mired and breathless

Bardolph. Out, alas, sir! cozenage...mere cozenage!

60 *Host.* Where be my horses? speak well of them, varletto.

Bardolph. Run away with the cozeners...for so soon as
I came beyond Eton, they threw me off, from behind one
of them, in a slough of mire...and set spurs, and away...
like three German devils...three Doctor Faustuses.

Host. They are gone but to meet the duke, villain. Do
not say, they be fled; Germans are honest men.

Sir HUGH EVANS opens the door and looks in

Evans. Where is mine host?

Host. What is the matter, sir?

Evans. Have a care of your entertainments: there is a
70 friend of mine come to town, tells me there is three
cozen-germans that has cozened all the hosts of Readins,
of Maidenhead, of Colebrook, of horses and money...I
tell you for good will, look you! you are wise, and full of
gibes and vlouting-stogs...and 'tis not convenient you
should be cozened! Fare you well.   [*he claps the door to*

Doctor CAIUS opens the door and looks in

Caius. Vere is mine host de Jarteer?

Host. Here, master doctor, in perplexity and doubtful
dilemma.

Caius. I cannot tell vat is dat: but it is tell-a me dat
80 you make grand preparation for a duke de Jarmany: by
my trot, dere is no duke, dat de court is know to come:
I tell you for good vill: adieu.   [*he claps the door to*

Host. Hue and cry, villain! go...Assist me, knight. I am
undone...Fly, run...hue and cry, villain! I am undone!
[*he runs forth with Bardolph after*

Falstaff. I would all the world might be cozened, for
I have been cozened and beaten too...If it should come

to the ear of the court, how I have been transformed...
and how my transformation hath been washed and
cudgelled, they would melt me out of my fat, drop by
drop, and liquor fishermen's boots with me: I warrant　90
they would whip me with their fine wits till I were as
crest-fallen as a dried pear...I never prospered since I
forswore myself at primero: well, if my wind were but
long enough [to say my prayers], I would repent...

Mistress QUICKLY enters

Now! whence come you?

Quickly. From the two parties, forsooth.

Falstaff. The devil take one party, and his dam the
other! and so they shall be both bestowed...I have
suffered more for their sakes—more than the villainous
inconstancy of man's disposition is able to bear.　100

Quickly. And have not they suffered? Yes, I warrant;
speciously one of them; Mistress Ford, good heart! is
beaten black and blue, that you cannot see a white spot
about her.

Falstaff. What, tell'st thou me of black and blue! I was
beaten myself into all the colours of the rainbow: and I
was like to be apprehended for the witch of Brainford.
But that my admirable dexterity of wit, my counter-
feiting the action of an old woman, delivered me, the
knave constable had set me i'th' stocks, i'th' common　110
stocks, for a witch.

Quickly. Sir: let me speak with you in your chamber,
you shall hear how things go, and I warrant to your
content...Here is a letter will say somewhat...Good
hearts, what ado here is to bring you together! Sure,
one of you does not serve heaven well, that you are so
crossed.

Falstaff. Come up into my chamber.　　[*they go up*

[4. 6.]   *HOST returns, with FENTON*

Host. Master Fenton, talk not to me,
My mind is heavy; I will give over all.
  Fenton. Yet hear me speak: assist me in my purpose,
And, as I am a gentleman, I'll give thee
A hundred pound in gold more than your loss.
  Host. I will hear you, Master Fenton; and I will at the
least keep your counsel.
  Fenton. From time to time I have acquainted you
With the dear love I bear to fair Anne Page,
10 Who mutually hath answered my affection,
So far forth as herself might be her chooser,
Even to my wish; I have a letter from her
Of such contents as you will wonder at;
The mirth whereof so larded with my matter,
That neither, singly, can be manifested,
Without the show of both: fat Falstaff
Hath a great scene; the image of the jest
I'll show you here at large. Hark, good mine host...
                              [*he peruses the letter*
To-night at Herne's oak, just 'twixt twelve and one,
20 Must my sweet Nan present the Fairy-Queen...
The purpose why, is here...in which disguise,
While other jests are something rank on foot,
Her father hath commanded her to slip
Away with Slender, and with him at Eton
Immediately to marry: she hath consented...
Now, sir,
Her mother, ever strong against that match
And firm for Doctor Caius, hath appointed
That he shall likewise shuffle her away,
30 While other sports are tasking of their minds,

And at the deanery, where a priest attends,
Straight marry her: to this her mother's plot
She seemingly obedient likewise hath
Made promise to the doctor...Now, thus it rests—
Her father means she shall be all in white;
And in that habit, when Slender sees his time
To take her by the hand and bid her go,
She shall go with him: her mother hath intended—
The better to denote her to the doctor,
For they must all be masked and vizarded—   40
That quaint in green she shall be loose enrobed,
With ribands pendent, flaring 'bout her head;
And when the doctor spies his vantage ripe,
To pinch her by the hand, and, on that token,
The maid hath given consent to go with him.

Host. Which means she to deceive? father or mother?

Fenton. Both, my good host, to go along with me:
And here it rests—that you'll procure the vicar
To stay for me at church, 'twixt twelve and one,
And, in the lawful name of marrying,   50
To give our hearts united ceremony.

Host. Well, husband your device; I'll to the vicar.
Bring you the maid, you shall not lack a priest.

Fenton. So shall I evermore be bound to thee;
.Besides, I'll make a present recompence.   [*they go out*

[5. 1.] *FALSTAFF and Mistress QUICKLY come
down from the chamber*

Falstaff. Prithee, no more prattling: go. I'll hold.
This is the third time: I hope good luck lies in odd
numbers...Away, go. They say there is divinity in odd
numbers, either in nativity, chance, or death...Away!

Quickly. I'll provide you a chain, and I'll do what I can
to get you a pair of horns.

Falstaff. Away, I say—time wears—hold up your head, and mince....   [*Mistress Quickly trips out; Ford enters*
How now, Master Brook! Master Brook, the matter will
10 be known to-night, or never....Be you in the Park about
midnight, at Herne's oak, and you shall see wonders.

Ford. Went you not to her yesterday, sir, as you told
me you had appointed?

Falstaff. I went to her, Master Brook, as you see, like
a poor old man, but I came from her, Master Brook, like
a poor old woman...That same knave Ford, her husband,
hath the finest mad devil of jealousy in him, Master
Brook, that ever governed frenzy....I will tell you he
beat me grievously, in the shape of a woman: for in the
20 shape of man, Master Brook, I fear not Goliath with a
weaver's beam, because I know also life is a shuttle. I am
in haste—go along with me—I'll tell you all, Master Brook
...[*donning his cloak*] Since I plucked geese, played truant,
and whipped top, I knew not what it was to be beaten,
till lately....[*at the door*] Follow me. I'll tell you strange
things of this knave Ford, on whom to-night I will be
revenged, and I will deliver his wife into your hand....
[*goes out*] Follow. Strange things in hand, Master Brook!
follow.   [*Ford follows, smiling*

[5.2.]   *The outskirts of Windsor Park; night*
PAGE, SHALLOW, *and* SLENDER *appear, with a lantern*

Page. Come, come; we'll couch i'th' castle-ditch till we
see the light of our fairies....Remember, son Slender, my
daughter.

Slender. Ay, forsooth—I have spoke with her, and we
have a nay-word how to know one another....I come to
her in white, and cry 'mum'; she cries 'budget,' and by
that we know one another.

Shallow. That's good too: but what needs either your 'mum' or her 'budget'? the white will decipher her well enough....It hath struck ten o'clock.   10

Page. The night is dark—light and spirits will become it well...Heaven prosper our sport! No man means evil but the devil, and we shall know him by his horns....Let's away; follow me.   [*they enter the Park*

[5. 3.]   *Mistress PAGE, Mistress FORD, and*
Doctor CAIUS come up

Mistress Page. Master doctor, my daughter is in green. When you see your time, take her by the hand, away with her to the deanery, and dispatch it quickly...Go before into the Park: we two must go together.

Caius. I know vat I have to do. Adieu.   [*he goes on*

Mistress Page. Fare you well, sir....My husband will not rejoice so much at the abuse of Falstaff as he will chafe at the doctor's marrying my daughter: but 'tis no matter; better a little chiding than a great deal of heart-break.

Mistress Ford. Where is Nan now, and her troop of fairies, and the Welsh †devil-hern?   10

Mistress Page. They are all couched in a pit hard by Herne's oak, with obscured lights; which at the very instant of Falstaff's and our meeting, they will at once display to the night.

Mistress Ford. That cannot choose but amaze him.

Mistress Page. If he be not amazed, he will be mocked; if he be amazed, he will every way be mocked.

Mistress Ford. We'll betray him finely.

Mistress Page. Against such lewdsters and their lechery
          Those that betray them do no treachery.   20

Mistress Ford. The hour draws on...To the oak, to the oak!   [*they enter the Park*

[5. 4.] *The Fairies approach, dancing, with masked lights:*
Sir HUGH EVANS, disguised as a Satyr in frieze and horns;
PISTOL attired as Puck; QUICKLY in white as Fairy-
Queen; ANNE PAGE with WILLIAM, and many other boys,
in red, black, grey, green and white

Evans. Trib, trib, fairies; come; and remember your
parts: be pold, I pray you; follow me into the pit; and
when I give the watch-'ords, do as I pid you...Come,
come—trib, trib.   [*they enter the Park*

[5. 5.]   *Beneath a mighty oak in Windsor Park*
      FALSTAFF disguised as Herne the hunter, 'with a
            buck's head upon him'

Falstaff. The Windsor bell hath struck twelve: the
minute draws on...Now, the hot-blooded gods assist me!
Remember, Jove, thou wast a bull for thy Europa—love
set on thy horns....O powerful love, that, in some respects, makes a beast a man; in some other, a man a
beast....You were also, Jupiter, a swan, for the love of
Leda...O omnipotent love, how near the god drew to
the complexion of a goose: a fault done first in the form
of a beast—O Jove, a beastly fault!—and then another
fault in the semblance of a fowl—think on't, Jove, a foul
10 fault! When gods have hot backs, what shall poor men
do? For me, I am here a Windsor stag, and the fattest,
I think, i'th' forest....Send me a cool rut-time, Jove, or
who can blame me to piss my tallow? Who comes here?
my doe?

      Mistress FORD comes from a thicket;
            Mistress PAGE following

Mistress Ford. Sir John? art thou there—my deer? my
male deer?

Falstaff. My doe with the black scut! Let the sky rain

potatoes; let it thunder to the tune of 'Green-sleeves,'
hail kissing-comfits, and snow eringoes; let there come   20
a tempest of provocation, I will shelter me here.
[he embraces her
  Mistress Ford. Mistress Page is come with me, sweetheart.

  Falstaff. Divide me like a bribed-buck, each a haunch:
I will keep my sides to myself, my shoulders for the fellow
of this walk—and my horns I bequeath your husbands!
Am I a woodman, ha? Speak I like Herne the hunter?
Why, now is Cupid a child of conscience—he makes
restitution....As I am a true spirit, welcome!
[' *there is a noise of horns*'
  Mistress Page. Alas! what noise?   30
  Mistress Ford. Heaven forgive our sins!
  Falstaff. What should this be?
  Mistress Ford, Mistress Page. Away, away!
[' *the two women run away*'
  Falstaff. I think the devil will not have me damned,
Lest the oil that's in me should set hell on fire;
—he would never else cross me thus.

*A sudden burst of light; the Fairies appear with crowns
of fire and rattles in their hands, led by a Satyr holding
a taper; they dance towards* FALSTAFF, *singing*

  Fairy-Queen. Fairies, black, grey, green, and white,
You moonshine revellers, and shades of night,
You orphan heirs of fixéd destiny,
Attend your office, and your quality....   40
Crier Hobgoblin, make the fairy oyes.
  Puck. Elves, list your names: silence, you airy toys....
[*they are still*
Crickét, to Windsor chimneys shalt thou leap;
Where fires thou find'st unraked and hearths unswept,

There pinch the maids as blue as bilberry.
Our radiant queen hates sluts and sluttery.
  Falstaff. They are fairies! he that speaks to them shall die.
I'll wink and couch: no man their works must eye.
                      [*he lies upon his face at the foot of the oak*
  Satyr. Where's Bead? Go you, and where you find
    a maid
50 That, ere she sleep, has thrice her prayers said,
  Raise up the organs of her fantasy,
  Sleep she as sound as careless infancy.
  But those as sleep and think not on their sins,
  Pinch them, arms, legs, backs, shoulders, sides, and shins.
    Fairy-Queen. About, about...
  Search Windsor Castle, elves, within and out....
  Strew good luck, ouphs, on every sacred room,
  That it may stand till the perpetual doom,
  In state as wholesome as in state 'tis fit,
60 Worthy the owner, and the owner it....
  The several chairs of order look you scour
  With juice of balm, and every precious flower:
  Each fair instalment, coat, and several crest,
  With loyal blazon, evermore be blest!
  And nightly, meadow-fairies, look you sing,
  Like to the Garter's compass, in a ring.
  Th'expressure that it bears, green let it be,
  More fertile-fresh than all the field to see;
  And, 'Honi soit qui mal y pense' write,
70 In emerald tufts, flowers purple, blue, and white—
  Like sapphire, pearl, and rich embroidery,
  Buckled below fair knighthood's bending knee:
  Fairies use flowers for their charáctery....
  Away, disperse! but till 'tis one o'clock,
  Our dance of custom round about the oak
  Of Herne the hunter, let us not forget.

Satyr. Pray you, lock hand in hand; yourselves in
      order set...   [*the Fairies encircle the oak*
And twenty glow-worms shall our lanterns be,
To guide our measure round about the tree....
But stay—I smell a man of middle earth.   80
Falstaff. Heavens defend me from that Welsh fairy,
Lest he transform me to a piece of cheese! ·
Puck. Vile worm, thou wast o'er-looked even in thy birth.
Fairy-Queen. With trial-fire touch me his finger-end:
If he be chaste, the flame will back descend,
And turn him to no pain; but if he start,
It is the flesh of a corrupted heart.
Puck. A trial, come!
Satyr [*setting his light to the buck's horns*]. Come: will
      this wood take fire?
            ['*they put the tapers to his fingers, and he starts*'
Falstaff. Oh, oh, oh!
Fairy-Queen. Corrupt, corrupt, and tainted in desire!   90
About him, fairies, sing a scornful rhyme—
And, as you trip, still pinch him to your time.

The Fairies dance about him and sing:

Fie on sinful fantasy: fie on lust and luxury:
Lust is but a bloody fire, kindled with unchaste desire,
      Fed in heart, whose flames aspire,
      As thoughts do blow them, higher and higher.
Pinch him, fairies, mutually: pinch him for his villainy.
      Pinch him, and burn him, and turn him about,
      Till candles, and star-light, and moon-shine be out.

As they sing, they pinch FALSTAFF. *Doctor* CAIUS *comes
one way, and steals away a fairy in green;* SLENDER *another
way, and takes off a fairy in white; and* FENTON *comes, and
steals away Mistress* ANNE PAGE. *A noise of hunting is
heard; and all the Fairies run away.* FALSTAFF *rises up,*

pulls off his buck's head, and would escape, but PAGE,
FORD, *Mistress* PAGE, *and Mistress* FORD *confront him.*

Page. Nay, do not fly! I think we have watched
100   you now...   [*Falstaff seeks to hide his face within
the buck's head once again*

Will none but Herne the hunter serve your turn?

Mistress Page. I pray you, come, hold up the jest
no higher.... [*Falstaff casts the buck's head from him*
Now, good Sir John, how like you Windsor wives?

[*pointing to the horns*

See you these, husband? do not these fair yokes
Become the forest better than the town?

Ford. Now, sir, who's a cuckold now?—Master Brook,
Falstaff's a knave, a cuckoldly knave—here are his horns,
Master Brook...And, Master Brook, he hath enjoyed
nothing of Ford's but his buck-basket, his cudgel, and
110   twenty pounds of money, which must be paid to Master
Brook—his horses are arrested for it, Master Brook.

Mistress Ford. Sir John, we have had ill luck; we could
never †mate...I will never take you for my love again
but I will always count you my deer.

Falstaff. I do begin to perceive that I am made an ass.

Ford. Ay, and an ox too: both the proofs are extant.

Falstaff. And these are not fairies! I was three or four
times in the thought they were not fairies—and yet the
guiltiness of my mind, the sudden surprise of my powers,
120   drove the grossness of the foppery into a received belief,
in despite of the teeth of all rhyme and reason, that they
were fairies....See now, how wit may be made a Jack-a-
lent, when 'tis upon ill employment!

Evans [*returns, without his satyr-mask*]. Sir John Falstaff,
serve Got, and leave your desires, and fairies will not
pinse you.

Ford. Well said, fairy Hugh.

Evans. And leave you your jealousies too, I pray you.

Ford. I will never mistrust my wife again, till thou art able to woo her in good English.　　130

Falstaff. Have I laid my brain in the sun, and dried it, that it wants matter to prevent so gross o'er-reaching as this? Am I ridden with a Welsh goat too? shall I have a coxcomb of frieze? 'tis time I were choked with a piece of toasted cheese.

Evans. Seese is not good to give putter; your pelly is all putter.

Falstaff. 'Seese' and 'putter'! Have I lived to stand at the taunt of one that makes fritters of English? This is enough to be the decay of lust and late-walking through　　140 the realm.

Mistress Page. Why, Sir John, do you think, though we would have thrust virtue out of our hearts by the head and shoulders, and have given ourselves without scruple to hell, that ever the devil could have made you our delight?

Ford. What, a hodge-pudding? a bag of flax?

Mistress Page. A puffed man?

Page. Old, cold, withered, and of intolerable entrails?

Ford. And one that is as slanderous as Satan?　　150

Page. And as poor as Job?

Ford. And as wicked as his wife?

Evans. And given to fornications, and to taverns, and sack, and wine, and metheglins, and to drinkings, and swearings and starings, pribbles and prabbles?

Falstaff. Well, I am your theme...you have the start of me, I am dejected...I am not able to answer the Welsh flannel. Ignorance itself is a plummet o'er me. Use me as you will.

Ford. Marry, sir, we'll bring you to Windsor, to one　　160 Master Brook, that you have cozened of money, to whom you should have been a pandar: over and above that you have suffered, I think to repay that money will be a biting affliction.

Page. Yet be cheerful, knight: thou shalt eat a posset to-night at my house, where I will desire thee to laugh at my wife, that now laughs at thee...Tell her Master Slender hath married her daughter.

Mistress Page. Doctors doubt that...[*aside*] If Anne
170 Page be my daughter, she is, by this, Doctor Caius' wife.

SLENDER *heard hulloing in the wood*

Slender. Whoa, ho, ho! father Page!

Page. Son, how now! how now, son! have you dispatched?

Slender [*comes up*]. Dispatched! I'll make the best in Gloucestershire know on't; would I were hanged, la, else.

Page. Of what, son?

Slender. I came yonder at Eton to marry Mistress Anne Page, and she's a great lubberly boy....If it had not been i'th' church, I would have swinged him, or he should
180 have swinged me....If I did not think it had been Anne Page, would I might never stir—and 'tis a postmaster's boy!

Page. Upon my life, then, you took the wrong.

Slender. What need you tell me that? I think so, when I took a boy for a girl...If I had been married to him, for all he was in woman's apparel, I would not have had him.

Page. Why, this is your own folly. Did not I tell you, how you should know my daughter—by her garments?

190 *Slender.* I went to her in white, and cried 'mum,' and she cried 'budget,' as Anne and I had appointed, and yet it was not Anne, but a postmaster's boy.

Mistress Page. Good George, be not angry. I knew of

your purpose...turned my daughter into green—and, indeed, she is now with the doctor at the deanery, and there married.

CAIUS heard calling wrathfully

Caius. Vere is Mistress Page? [*comes up*] By gar, I am cozened! I ha' married un garçon, a boy; un paysan, by gar....a boy! it is not Anne Page—by gar, I am cozened!
Mistress Page. Why! did you take her in green?   200
Caius. Ay, by gar, and 'tis a boy: by gar, I'll raise all Windsor!   [*he hurries away, shaking his fist*
Ford. This is strange...Who hath got the right Anne?
Page. My heart misgives me—here comes Master Fenton....

FENTON and ANNE PAGE appear, arm in arm

How now, Master Fenton!
Anne [*kneels*]. Pardon, good father! good my mother, pardon!
Page. Now, Mistress! how chance you went not with Master Slender?
Mistress Page. Why went you not with master doctor, maid?   210
Fenton. You do amaze her...Hear the truth of it.
You would have married her most shamefully,
Where there was no proportion held in love...
The truth is, she and I—long since contracted—
Are now so sure that nothing can dissolve us...
Th'offence is holy that she hath committed,
And this deceit loses the name of craft,
Of disobedience or unduteous title,
Since therein she doth evitate and shun
A thousand irreligious cursèd hours,   220
Which forcèd marriage would have brought upon her.

Ford. Stand not amazed. Here is no remedy:
In love, the heavens themselves do guide the state—
Money buys lands, and wives are sold by fate. ·

Falstaff. I am glad, though you have ta'en a special
stand to strike at me, that your arrow hath glanced.

Page. Well, what remedy? Fenton, heaven give
     thee joy!
What cannot be eschewed, must be embraced.

Falstaff. When night-dogs run, all sorts of deer
     are chased.

Mistress Page. Well, I will muse no further...
230   Master Fenton,
Heaven give you many, many merry days!
Good husband, let us every one go home,
And laugh this sport o'er by a country fire—
Sir John and all.

Ford.   Let it be so. Sir John,
To Master Brook you yet shall hold your word,
For he to-night shall lie with Mistress Ford.

                              [*they troop homeward*

THE COPY FOR *THE MERRY WIVES OF WINDSOR*, 1623

AND ITS RELATION TO THAT FOR THE BAD QUARTO, 1602

An editor of *The Merry Wives* has to reckon with two texts, both imperfect, though differing greatly in quality and authority: the Bad Quarto of 1602 and the Folio text of 1623. Bibliographically, the latter appears to belong to the same category as *The Two Gentlemen*; that is to say, it contains (*a*) no stage-directions of any kind, (*b*) no exits beyond the general 'exit' or 'exeunt' at the end of the scenes, and (*c*), with the single exception to be noted shortly, no entries except a list at the head of each scene of the characters appearing within it, in the order of their appearance. On grounds discussed at length in our edition of *The Two Gentlemen* (v. pp. 77–8), we account for these anomalies on the supposition that the 'copy' for the Folio text was made up by stringing together players' parts with the aid of the theatrical 'plot' of the play; and it is unnecessary to repeat those arguments here.

There is, however, one marked difference between these two plays which needs a word of comment. We found *The Two Gentlemen* singularly free from small textual ambiguities (though certainly not from wholesale corruption), and we offered a two-fold explanation of this: the simplicity of language in an early play, and the likelihood that verbal ambiguities would not be tolerated in players' parts. How then does *The Merry Wives*, also we believe derived from players' parts, come to be strewn with verbal cruxes? The answer, in our view, is again a two-fold one. First, the vocabulary of *The Merry Wives* is unusually difficult, how much more difficult than that of *The Two Gentlemen* may be seen by comparing the lengths of the glossaries to the two plays in this edition; and obviously the more difficult the vocabulary the wider the margin of possible error. In the second place, the clearing up of ambiguities in players' parts takes time; it involves careful transcript, careful conning of the parts by the actors and at least several rehearsals. Now, if tradition be believed, and we see every reason for believing it, time was a very scarce commodity when *The Merry Wives* was taking shape as the received text. A royal command to the Chamberlain's men for a play upon 'Falstaff in love,' within fourteen days, is enough of itself to account for all the imperfections of the Folio version. Lack of time, also, may possibly account for the use of players' parts as 'copy,' seeing that prompt-copy, revised under conditions of such stress, is likely to have been too difficult a manuscript for a printer to tackle. The recorded Jacobean Court performance (v. p. xxi *n*.), however, offers an alternative explanation, namely that the prompt-copy was abridged for this occasion in such a way that it presented a text different from the one which had become popular upon the common stage and which therefore readers of the Folio would expect to find therein. In any event, it seems that when the Folio was taken in hand little beyond the original players' parts was forthcoming for this text, though the single internal entry (at 5. 5. 37) leaves us wondering whether the fairy-dialogue in the last scene may have been set up from a scrap of author's manuscript.

With the Bad Quarto of 1602 (v. pp. x–xii) we are here concerned only in so far as it may be used to piece out the imperfections of the Folio text. Garbled as the Quarto is, even the most fastidious of editors have been unable altogether to give it the cold shoulder, for the

simple reason that without recourse to it some of the
Folio speeches are quite unintelligible. In other words,
as we believe, little scraps of dialogue were inadvertently
omitted in the hasty transcription of the parts¹ for the
command performance and some of these can be restored
from the Quarto. But editors have rightly been very
chary in drawing upon a text, as to the nature and origin
of which they were completely in the dark. The bolder
course we have pursued in the present edition is to be
set down to our belief that this darkness has now been
in large measure dissipated.

Corners of the problem still remain obscure, but it
is safe to say that we know in general terms how the
'copy' for the Quarto was made up. Parts of it were
'reported,' that is to say written out from memory,
by a pirate-actor, who, as Dr Greg has shown, played
the Host in the final version. But reporting will not
account for everything. It will not account for the
verse-scenes in the Quarto, which are different both in
style and matter from those in the Folio, and despite
the poverty of the verse (incidentally not greatly in-
ferior to that of the 1623 text) are quite beyond the
scope of the pirate, who in other parts of the Quarto
is hardly able to write decent prose. It will not account
for the famous 'garmombles' passage and others which
are not in the Folio and clearly derive from an earlier
version. Finally, it will not account for certain links of
material transmission between the two texts, which—
faint and scanty though they may be—indicate that the
'copy' for the Quarto was at least in part transcribed
from the same manuscript which, after revision, provided
the materials for the authoritative text. Consider, for
example, the Quarto and Folio versions of the following
speech, taken from 2. 2. 5–12.

(Q.)   *Fal.* Not a pennie: I haue beene content you
        fhuld lay my countenance to pawne: I haue grated
        vpon my good friends for 3. repriues, for you and

your Coach-fellow *Nym*, elſe you might a looked
thorow a grate like a geminy of baboones. I am damned in hell for ſwearing to Gentlemen your good
ſouldiers and tall fellowes: And when miſtriſſe *Briget* loſt the handle of her Fan, I tooked on my ho-
thou hadſt it not[1].

(F.)   *Fal.* Not a penny: I haue beene content (Sir,) you
ſhould lay my countenance to pawne: I haue grated vpon my good friends for three Repreeues for you, and
your Coach-fellow *Nim*; or elſe you had look'd through
the grate, like a Geminy of Baboones: I am damn'd in
hell, for ſwearing to Gentlemen my friends, you were
good Souldiers, and tall-fellowes. And when Miſtreſſe
Briget loſt the handle of her Fan, I took't vpon mine honour thou hadſt it not.

The punctuation, apart from the commas, is practically
identical, and identity of punctuation is a powerful
clue, while spellings and capitals coincide in words like
'pawne,' 'Coach-fellow,' 'Gentlemen,' '*Briget*,' 'Fan.'
There is even a striking similarity in the distribution
of the lines. In a word, the evidence suggests that the
texts at this point go back to the same manuscript source,
such variations as occur being due to carelessness in
copying out the parts, which here seemingly lie behind
both versions.

Considerations like these, taken in conjunction with
others of a more literary character with which one of
us deals in the Introduction (v. pp. x–xxvii) and the
other elsewhere in collaboration with Mr A. W. Pollard
(see below for reference), render us confident that the
1602 Quarto possesses a higher authority than has hitherto been suspected, that in fact the 'copy' consisted partly
of an abridged playhouse version (probably in the form
of players' parts) of an old play which had not yet been
brought by revision into its final shape, and partly of
additions made thereto by the pirate-actor who was
responsible for the surreptitious publication.

[1] The second syllable of 'honour' is omitted in the Q.

Such a text, if used with due caution, may be of great service to an editor who has to deal with an *editio princeps* in the sorry condition of *The Merry Wives* of 1623. With the knowledge that any given passage in the Quarto derives at best ultimately from the same manuscript, albeit un-revised, as provided the players' parts for the final version, and at worst from an actor who played an important part in that final version, he is at liberty to draw upon it in order to fill up the gaps in the Folio text. We have, however, proceeded with circumspection in this matter, have included no passage from the Quarto which does not materially assist, in our view, the under-standing of the Folio context, and have enclosed all such additions, even down to single words, within square brackets, so that the reader may realise exactly where he stands.

The Quarto again has hitherto proved a stumbling-block in the matter of those verbal cruxes, or misprints, referred to above. Ignorant of the provenance of the texts they were handling, previous editors have generally and properly shrunk from emendation in passages where both agree, even when the reading cries out for recti-fication. A comparison, however, of the Bad and Good Quartos of *Hamlet* has shown that in texts derived from the same manuscript common misprints are quite likely to occur[1]. On the other hand, where the possibility of 'reporting' has to be reckoned with, an error in the players' parts of the final version repeated on the stage is also likely to be reproduced by the pirate. A single example will make the position clear. At 1. 3. 28 Nym, replying to Falstaff's 'His filching was like an unskilful singer, he kept not time,' exclaims 'The good humour is to steal at a minute's rest'; and both texts of *The Merry Wives* give this reading. Now, the reference to 'an unskilful singer' and to 'time,' together with the

[1] J. Dover Wilson, *The Copy for Hamlet*, 1603, etc.

parallel at *Rom.* 2. 4. 22, 'his minim-rest, one, two and the third in your bosom,' makes it certain, we contend, that 'a minim-rest' is the true reading here. 'Minute's rest' is pointless—sixty seconds are fifty-nine too many for Nym's context; but 'a minim-rest,' i.e. (*a*) the shortest rest in music, and (*b*) the flourish of the cut-throat's weapon, is precisely the meaning required. 'Minute's,' however, is not likely to be a mis*print* for 'minim,' and the scene in which the passage occurs in the Quarto bears all the marks of the reporter's hand. We, therefore, attribute the Folio corruption to a mis-correction by a player who could not read (or could not understand) the word which stood in his part. And whether 'a minute's rest' in the Quarto comes from a manuscript source or from the pirate's memory, its agreement with the Folio does not frighten us; we are convinced that both texts are wrong, and emend accordingly.

The Folio text, then, is a revision of the same manuscript which lies, at whatever remove and however garbled and abridged, at the back of the Quarto version. With the larger implications of this fact we deal in our Introduction. Here we have briefly to note the textual and bibliographical features connected with it. The revision was hasty and incomplete (v. pp. xii–xix). Haste is evident in many directions. For example, there are those imperfections of the text, the missing words and phrases, the verbal obscurities and corruptions, already noticed. The 'Broom-Brook,' 'bully-rook' and 'Herne-Horn' puzzles probably arose from the same cause (v. notes 2. 1. 193; 1. 3. 3; 4. 4. 28). That lack of time forbade a complete revision is equally clear. The horse-stealing plot was *de trop*, and yet the revisers were unable to do more than tear it out of the text, leaving loose threads behind (v. note 4. 3. 1–2). Falstaff is a composite character, within whose mighty girdle we find at times the sententious philanderer moving most uneasily (v. notes 1. 3. 3; 2. 1. 51–5; 2. 2. 168; 5. 5. 117–23). The figure of Justice Shallow, who takes the centre of the stage in the opening scene, becomes more and more attenuated as the drama proceeds; the deer-stealing plot is left in mid-air; at one point Master Ford has to step into his worship's shoes to keep the dialogue afloat (v. note 2. 1. 191); and finally we lose the old man altogether in Windsor Forest. Again, it was obviously the original intention of the revisers, and of Shakespeare in particular we may suppose, to link up this Falstaff play with the rest of the Prince Hal cycle; but the intention was never carried through. We catch a glimpse of Pistol in pursuit of Widow Quickly (2. 2. 127–9); we are given to understand that Fenton was one of Hal's boon-companions (3. 2. 65)—and we are left to surmise the rest as best we can. Queen Elizabeth had laughed over Falstaff in *Henry IV* and desired to see him 'in love'; but the 'fourteen days' allowed were all too short for the full conversion of the old play into a new chapter in the cycle. The revision begins well, but grows more and more fitful as the text proceeds.

It is peculiarly difficult to produce bibliographical evidence, which depends largely upon disturbance in verse-arrangement, in support of revision in a play mainly written in prose. But *The Merry Wives* contains four verse-scenes, and these are full of the recognised clues. We are not surprised to find that Fenton, who 'speaks holiday,' should be given verse-speeches; yet the scenes in which he appears come mostly in the second half of the play, where the revision *ex hypothesi* was hurried and superficial, and it is noteworthy that at his first entrance early in the play (1. 4. 130 *et seq.*) he talks prose. Still more remarkable is the fact that his presence on the stage seems to make the most unexpected persons break forth into verse likewise; in 3. 4. both Master and Mistress Page address him in verse, while in 4. 6. the Host himself turns poet. Nor are the Fenton scenes the only ones in which verse is found. Prose and verse are quite irrationally blended in 4. 4., and a reference to our notes upon this scene will show that the marks of revision are patent throughout. Lastly in 5. 5. we have that curious alternation of prose and verse, section by section, which we noted in 2. 1. of *The Tempest* (v. p. 84) as characteristic of partial or composite revision. It will be observed that in one of these verse-sections even Falstaff himself speaks verse (v. note 5. 5. 37–105). Thus the bibliographical evidence, like that of the plot-structure above noted, indicates that the revision was far more hurried in the second than in the first half of the play. It suggests, in other words, that the original drama, if not wholly in verse, contained many more verse-scenes than the text as we have it, and that it was the intention of the revisers to rewrite the whole thing in prose, except perhaps the fairy-episode in 5. 5., an intention which lack of time forbade them to realise.

Here, however, we are confronted with an interesting and, at first sight, somewhat disconcerting fact. The verse-scenes in the Folio are full of the marks of revision, abridgment and adaptation, as we have seen. But the verse itself differs considerably, quite apart from these alterations, from that in the Quarto, that is to say the Quarto verse had been rewritten before the Folio revision was taken in hand. In other words, it took *two* revisions to convert the manuscript which lies behind the Quarto into the text which the Folio gives us. We have assumed, we believe with propriety, that the second of these revisions was that which took place at the time of the command performance. The question of the first revision raises the whole problem of the history of *The Merry Wives* text, which is beyond the scope of the present enquiry.

A good deal of work has been done upon these texts, and the student may find it useful to be referred to the following books and articles, some of which have been used in the foregoing paragraphs, or in the notes that follow:

F. G. Fleay, *Life of Shakespeare*, pp. 112, 210–14. 1886.

P. A. Daniel, *Merry Wives of Windsor*, 1602 (Introd.). Griggs Facsimile. 1888.

H. C. Hart, *Merry Wives of Windsor* (Introd.), Arden Shakespeare. 1904.

W. W. Greg, *Shakespeare's Merry Wives of Windsor*, 1602. Oxford, 1910.

J. M. Robertson, *The Problem of 'The Merry Wives.'* Shakespeare Association. 1917.

A. W. Pollard and J. Dover Wilson, *The Stolne and Surreptitious Shakespearian Texts*. Times Literary Supplement, Aug. 7, 1919.

1921   D.W.

P.S. [1954]. The foregoing Note on the Copy, written a generation ago, is almost completely out of date, though what the coincidences and differences between Q. and F., there observed, actually signify has not yet been determined. In addition to the publications 1924–38 mentioned on p. xxxix above, readers may be referred to W. W. Greg, *The Editorial Problem in Shakespeare*, 1942 [2nd ed. 1951], pp. 70–2. As the Q. was edited by Sir Walter Greg his opinions, always authoritative, have a special claim to our respect on this text.

NOTES

All significant departures from the Folio are recorded, the name of the critic who first suggested a reading being placed in brackets. Illustrative spellings and misprints are quoted from the Good Quarto texts or from the Folio where no Good Quarto exists. The line-numeration for reference to plays not yet issued in this edition is that used in Bartlett's *Concordance*.

F., unless otherwise specified, stands for the First Folio and Q. for the Quarto of 1602; T.I. and Facs.=the Textual Introduction and the Facsimile of a passage from the 'Shakespearian' Addition to *Sir Thomas More*, both to be found in the *Tempest* volume; N.E.D.= *The New English Dictionary*; Sh. Eng.= *Shakespeare's England*; S.D.= Stage-direction; G.= Glossary; Daniel = *Time-Analysis of the plots of Shakespeare's Plays*, P. A. Daniel, New Shak.Soc. For Hart, Greg, Robertson, Pollard, etc. v. p. 101..

Characters in the Play. The F. gives no list of 'The Names of all the Actors,' perhaps because the text finishes close to the foot of a page. We have borrowed 'Shallow, a country justice' and 'irregular humorists' from the F. list at the end of 2 *Hen. IV*, while 'his wise cousin' comes from the title-page of the Q. For 'Nym' v. G. and p. xxxii.

Acts and Scenes. Regularly divided in F.; but probably taken from the 'plot,' v. T.I., § 3. In our arrangement, we have avoided any change of place except where the text clearly demands one.

Punctuation. Crude, but on the whole surprisingly careful considering the carelessness of the text in other respects. We have occasionally printed a colon for a semi-colon and *vice versa* or an exclamation-mark for a colon. Other and more important changes are recorded in the Notes.

Stage-directions. None in F. We have taken a few from Q., placing them in inverted commas, v. p. 93.

Glossary. In order to relieve the Notes for this difficult text, all exegetic matter possible has been relegated to the G., which it is hoped the reader will consult freely.

I. I.

2. *Star-chamber* v. G. We hear nothing more of Shallow's quarrel with Falstaff after this scene; v. pp. xiii–xiv, 99, and notes 2. 1. 191; 4. 4. 1; 5. 2. 8.

14. *dozen white luces* v. Introd. pp. xxxv–xxxvii. The Lucy arms, according to Camden, were 'three Luces Argent in a shield gules.'

20. *cod* F. 'Coate' The F. reading has been hitherto unexplained. There is clearly corruption and Evans' pronunciation appears to be at the bottom of it. Note: (i) 'cod' makes excellent sense in Shallow's speech, since 'luce' was a term applied not only to the fresh-water pike but also, though according to Shallow incorrectly, to the salt-water cod or hake (v. N.E.D.). (ii) As Evans made no difference between *d* and *t*, Shallow apparently imagined that the parson was speaking of 'cod' and perhaps even suspected him of a 'salt' jest (cf. 'codpiece'). (iii) Not understanding all this, the compositor or transcriber seems to have taken 'cod' or 'codd' in Shallow's speech as a mistake for 'coat' or 'cote.' Cf. *A.Y.L.* 2. 4. 50, n.

30. *compromises* F. 'compremifes'—which most edd. follow, taking it as a mispronunciation—is only a Shakespearian spelling; cf. *M.V.* 1. 3. 79 'compremyz'd.'

31. *it is a riot* v. G. 'Star-chamber.' For a fight between two men constituting a riot see *Troublesome Reign* 1. 1. 75–82. [1954.]

32–3. *the council...the fear of Got* Evans, with his head full of the 'atonements and compromises' of 'the Church,' imagines that Shallow is speaking of an ecclesiastical 'council' or synod.

38. *swort* F. 'Sword' The quibble upon 'sort'

(= issue, upshot) shows that a *t* was intended. Evans'
'part' is most inconsistent in its use of *d* and *t*. We have
restored the *t* throughout. Cf. note 1.4.70.

41. *Thomas* Page is elsewhere called 'George'—one
of the many signs of hasty revision.

53, 56. *Did her grandsire* etc. *I know* etc. F. gives
these two speeches to Slender. Capell restored them to
Shallow, and Malone approved. N.B. The second speech
cannot be Slender's after his words at ll. 43–4.

78. *ill killed* Venison drained of blood, because
the deer was badly wounded some hours before being
killed [1954].

87. *fault* This has puzzled many; but v. G.

91. *good and fair* v. G.

106. *But not kissed* etc. This looks like a reference to
some lost ballad, possibly on the deer-stealing incident
of 1590; v. G. 'Star-chamber.'

118–19. *They carried...my pocket* Cf. l. 142 'pick
Master Slender's purse' which makes it certain that the
F. text has omitted a sentence corresponding with that
we have inserted here from Q.

124. *Slice* v. G. Farmer gives 'pauca, pauca' to
Evans, perhaps rightly.

131–3. *fidelicet Master Page* etc. The F. brackets
are expressive here. 133. *Garter* F. 'Gater'

145. *seven groats in mill-sixpences* v. G. 'groat.'

147. *Yed* F. 'Yead' i.e. Edward; cf. 'Yedward,'
1 *Henry IV*, 1.2.149.

150–3. *Ha, thou...liest!* Printed as prose in F. This
suggests revision in the original MS, and the first line
has clearly been 'adapted.'

163. *sentences* v. G.

165. *being fap* N.E.D. and edd. interpret as 'being
drunk,' though no other instance of 'fap' is known,
except one of 1818 which probably derives from this.
We believe the word to be corrupt, and that Bardolph

was intended to say *being fox* or *foxed* i.e. drunk, v. O.E.D. 'fox' vb. 2 [corrected in 1954]. For 'cashier' and 'careers' v. G.

203. *Nay, I will do* etc. Slender evidently thinks that the 'tender' concerned the 'cashiering,' and is irritated with Evans, the peacemaker.

222. *carry-her* v. G. 'carry.'

233. *contempt* (Theobald) F. 'content'

236. *fall* Possibly mispronunciation, possibly misprint of 'falt,' a 16th cent. spelling.

268. *he hot my shin* Slender jests feebly, as he would. The insertion from the Q. alone makes the reference to 'hot meat' intelligible. Slender is, of course, quite unconscious of the connexion between 'hot meat' and 'stewed prunes' (v. G.). 'Hot' was an obsolete, and provincial (v. *Dial. Dict.* 'hit'), past tense of 'hit.'

273. *quarrel at it* etc. As a puritan, Slender was bound to decry bear-baiting though he loved the sport well.

295. *I'll rather be unmannerly* etc. A saying in the West Country to-day.

I. 2.

1. *Doctor Caius* The English Dr Caius (1510–1573), founder of Gonville and Caius College, Cambridge, was the most renowned English physician of the century and it is remarkable to find his name used for a French physician (v. *Shakespeare and Dr Caius*, A. D. McNair, *The Caian*, vol. xxviii). It is conceivable that the character was intended as a caricature of the Englishman in an earlier draft of the play and that he was converted into a Frenchman in a subsequent revision. But cf. p. xxxiii.

11. *seese* (Dyce) F. 'Cheefe' Cf. 5. 5. 136, where F. reads 'Seefe'

I. 3.

3. *bully-rook* v. G. 'bully.' 'Rook,' which = (*a*) the castle at chess (Steevens), (*b*) a sharper, would be an

appropriate nickname for Oldcastle (v. p. xxiv, and note
4. 5. 6). That it is applied elsewhere to other characters
was perhaps due to the hasty revision, when the original
point had been forgotten.

scholarly and wisely The references to Falstaff's scholarship in this play are remarkable (cf. 1. 3. 48; 2. 2. 168,
213; 4. 5. 53–8) and are, we believe, traces of the sententious hero of the old play (cf. pp. xxiv–xxv).

15. *lime* (Q.) F. '*liue*' Cf. G. 'froth and lime'.

17. *old cloak...jerkin* Prov.; v. Tilley, B607.

28. *a minim-rest* F. and Q. 'a minutes reſt,' v.
pp. 97–8. Singer reads 'minim's.'

29. *Convey,* F. 'Convey:'

35. *ravens* v. G.

48. *studied her well,* (Q.) F. 'ſtudied her will;'

49. *into English* Pistol seems to be quibbling upon
'ingle'= to cuddle. 'Inglis' or 'Ingles' was a common
sp. of 'English' at this period.

50. *anchor* v. G. Kinnear conjectures 'angle,' which
is attractive in view of 'English' (l. 49), 'angels' (l. 52)
and 'the humour rises' (l. 55)—possibly 'anchor' was
a player's makeshift for a word he could not read;
cf. p. 98.

52. *a legion* (Pope and all mod. edd.) F. 'a legend'
Q. 'legians.' As 'legend' and 'legion' could apparently
be used interchangeably at this period (cf. N.E.D.
'legend,' 7*b*); Falstaff may be quibbling on 'the
Golden Legend.' [1954.]

53. *As many devils* etc. i.e. Falstaff is a legion of devils
in himself. For 'entertain' and 'boy' v. G.

59. *œillades* F. 'illiads' Cf. *Lear* 4. 5. 25 'Eliads,' the
only other example in Shakespeare.

62. *the sun on dunghill* Cf. *Ham.* 2. 2. 181.

66. *Here's another letter* etc. Falstaff has already said
this in ll. 57–8; the repetition is probably due to hasty
revision.

75. *And by my side wear steel* i.e. 'and I a soldier!'

82. *learn the humour* (Q.) F. 'learne the honor'

83. *skirted page* With this hint as to Robin's costume cf. 3. 2. 16; 3. 3. 24, 31. F. and Q. read 'Page'

84–5. *holds,* F. 'holds:' *poor:* F. 'poor,'

85. *high and low* v. G.

90. *star* F. 'Star' Q. reads 'Fairies' which we take to be a misprint for 'fair eyes' i.e. the stars.

91. *With both the humours* i.e. his own 'wit' and Page's 'steel.'

92, 93, 97. *Page...Ford...Page* (Q.) F. 'Ford...Page... Ford' Cf. 2. 1. 99 *et seq.* There is something to be said for the F. reading, which all mod. edd. reject, since Nym's second speech would be far more appropriate to Ford than to Page. The mistake, or confusion, was probably due to hasty revision.

95. *prove,* F. 'proue;'

98. *with' yellows* F. 'with yallowneffe'; Q. 'with Iallowes' The Q. reading is clearly the better (v. G. 'yellows' and following note), and 'Iallowes,' with a minim too many (v. T.I. p. xli), might easily be taken for 'Iallownes.'

99. *mind* (Jackson) F. 'mine'—an *e:d* error. Malone and Steevens read 'mien.' Cf. *Two Gent.* 3. 2. 59 'And cannot soon revolt and change your mind'; *L.L.L.* 5. 2. 74 'gravity's revolt to wantonness'; *Tw. Nt.* 2. 4. 102 'surfeit, cloyment and revolt,' from which it is evident that 'revolt' is often used by Shakespeare in the sense of a sudden revulsion of mind or feeling.

100. *malcontents* F. 'Malecontents' Cf. *Two Gent.* note 2. 1. 19.

I. 4.

20. *whey-face* (Capell) F. 'wee-face'; Q. (which is clearly reported here) gives us 'a whay coloured beard'! —which shows, however, that 'whey' stuck in the pirate's memory. Hart writes: '"Wee" seems to have been hardly in use in the south at the beginning of the 17th

cent. except in the phrase of distance, "a wee bit."' We
have 'whay-face' again in *Macb.* 5. 3. 18.

21. *cane-coloured* (Rowe) F. 'Caine colourd'; Q. 'kane
coloured' Steevens and Malone took 'cane-coloured'
as meaning 'yellow' like a cane. (Cf. *M.N.D.* 1. 2. 95
'straw-colour beard.') Theobald read 'Cain' and supposed a reference to the traditional colour of Cain's beard
in the tapestries. But 'cane' may mean 'weasel' (v.
N.E.D., which however gives no instance earlier than
Gilbert White); and a whey-face, with a weasel-beard,
makes a perfect vignette of Slender.

40. *And down* etc. A popular refrain or burthen of
the period. Cf. *Ham.* 4. 5. 170.

42. *un boitier vert* F. 'vnboyteene verd'; Rowe
emended 'un boitier,' and Dyce 'vert'; 'boyteene' was
no doubt 'boyteere' in the original (a minim-error).
N.B. The French in this text was apparently written in
16th cent. phonetic spelling to assist the players, and is
printed in italics in F., which suggests that it was written
in 'Italian' script in Caius' part; cf. notes ll. 48, 51, 61;
5. 5. 198.

44. *green-a* F. 'greene-a' Caius, being French, pro-
nounces final mute *e*, sometimes even in words which are
without it. We omit the *e* before his -*a* throughout; cf.
'tak-a' (F. 'take-a') l. 56.

48. *ma foi* etc. (Rowe) F. 'mai foy, il fait for ehando,
Ie man voi a le Court la grand affaires'—a pretty blend
of phonetic spelling and misprint!

51. *dépêche Quickly* (Rowe) F. 'de-peech quickly'

61. *Qu'ai-j'oublié* (Johnson) F. 'que ay ie oublie'

67. *laroon* (F.) i.e. 'robber, thief' (N.E.D.). Mod. edd.
give the Fr. form 'larron,' possibly rightly, though Caius'
French was not his strongest point.

70. *Verefore* (Hanmer) F. 'Wherefore,' which however
prints 'vherefore' at 3. 1. 77. Caius' pronunciation like
that of Evans (v. note 1. 1. 38) is inconsistently rendered
by F. We see no point in reproducing, or recording, these

inconsistencies. Cf. F. 'what' 1. 4. 72 with 'vat' at
2. 3. 3.

86. *baillez* (Theobald) F. 'ballow' As z and w are
very different letters in 'English' script, the error is
curious. Possibly the original gave 'ballecici' (= baillez
ici), which provides four minims for the three in w;
cf. *Hen. V* (Q1) sc. viii 'venecia' misp. for 'venez ici.'

91. *do your* (Capell) F. 'doe yoe your'

109. *stones* v. G.

110. *trow* (F2) F. 'throw'; F. reads 'troat' at l. 106.

118. S.D. *he boxes her ears* Quickly's sudden exclamation 'What the good-jer!' (i.e. 'What the devil!') and
Caius' remark about turning 'her head out of door' make
some such S.D. necessary.

123. S.D. *the door shuts* Daniel, as quoted by Aldis
Wright, reads 'You shall have Anne—[*exeunt Caius and
Rugby*]—fool's head of your own.'

145. *such another Nan* v. G.

2. I.

1. *have I 'scaped* (F2) F. 'haue fcap'd'

5. *precisian* (F.) Johnson conj. 'physician' and has
been followed by most edd. But 'precisian,' e.g. a puritan
minister, gives good sense. Love is King, with court-
chaplain and privy council. *councillor* F. 'Counsailour'
v. note *Temp.* 1. 1. 20. Falstaff says, in effect, 'though
Love receives admonition from Reason, he does not ask
his advice before taking a line of action.'

17–27. *What a Herod* etc. The printing of these lines
in the F. is of bibliographical interest. The compositor,
or copyist, first takes them as verse, and accordingly
begins each line with a capital; as he proceeds it dawns
upon him that he is dealing with prose—the lines begin
to run right across the column, and finally in the last
two the initial capitals are dropped. It is evident that,
at any rate at this point, the 'copy' was written in short
lengths, which suggests players' parts. Cf. *Two Gent.*
note 1. 1. 133–7.

20. *with the devil's name!* This is curious. Possibly 'name' is an error for 'neiue,' i.e. neif, fist. F3 reads 'i'th' for 'with.'

31. *You look very ill* v. G. 'ill.'

46. *back* v. G.

51–5. *yet he would not swear...truth of his words* Hart comments: 'Mrs Ford's description of Falstaff here does not seem to be meant to be humorous. It is so astonishing that it reads like an extract from another play.' We agree, and take the passage to be a fossil from the old play, before the hero was re-named Falstaff, v. p. xxiv, and Pollard; cf. also notes 2. 2. 168; 5. 5. 117–23.

52. *praised* (Theobald) F. 'praiſe'—an *e:d* error.

56. *Hundredth Psalm* (Rowe) F. 'hundred Pſalms' 'Hundred' was a common 16th cent. sp. of 'hundredth' (cf. *Ham.* 1. 2. 238), and the compositor has taken it as 'hundred' here—wrongly.

88. *pawned his horses* This is somehow related to 5. 5. 111 'his horses are arrested for it'; but the connecting thread has been broken, or not carried through, in revision, probably owing to the excision of the horse-stealing plot. N.B. It is the sole indication before 4. 3. that the Host kept a stable. Cf. note 4. 3. 1–2.

103–9. *He wooes both high and low* etc. Pistol's first speech is printed as prose, and his second is misdivided, in F. Perhaps due to confusion of lining in the 'part'; cf. note ll. 17–27.

108. *Like Sir Actæon be* (Gould) F. 'Like Sir *Acteon* he' Initial *h* and *b* are often confused, for some reason, in the Qq. (e.g. 'he' for 'be' 2 *Hen. IV*. 3. 2. 353). For 'Actæon' v. G.

114. F. 'Away ſir Corporall *Nim*:/Beleeue it (*Page*) he ſpeakes ſence.' Many attempts at emendation. If we take '(*Page*)' as a S.D. which has crept into the text, the difficulty is solved, and a sixfooter emerges. The Q. reading '*Page* belieue him what he ſes' (obviously

reported) suggests that the mistake was due to the players, not to the F. compositor.

115. *I will be patient* N.B. Ford speaks verse. Cf. p. 99.

121–2. *My name is Corporal Nym* etc. F., followed by all edd., prints these lines as prose; they are in the same metre as Pistol's above. Taken with Ford's isolated verse-line (115), they raise the question whether the whole scene was not originally in verse.

123. *bread and cheese* v. G.

124. *and there's the humour of it* Not absolutely neces-sary to the sense, but all edd. since Capell have adopted it from the Q.

126. *English* (F.) Q. 'humor' which Pope and Malone read.

131. *priest o' th' town*=parish priest.

132. S.D. *having heard all* Mrs Ford's conduct here and Mrs Page's at 3. 2. 9–27 prove that they have over-heard Pistol's words and noted their effect upon Ford. This would, of course, be made clear upon the stage.

140. *head now...Will* F. 'head,/Now: will' In this and surrounding speeches the compositor, or copyist, is uncertain whether he is dealing with prose or verse (cf. notes ll. 17–27, 103–9), and finding 'now' at the beginning of a line, he gives it a capital. Many edd., ignoring the F. pointing, have fallen into the trap and read 'head. Now will' Cf. note 3. 3. 65.

177. *Good even* v. G. This is one of the few errors of time in the text. It is early morning. v. p. xvii. Note the commas in this speech, indicative of lack of breath.

191. *None, I protest* etc. This is given to Shallow in F., though not in Q. (which is here obviously reported). Ford, of course, must be speaking; but note (i) the Host's question is pointless as addressed to him, (ii) 'suit' can only refer to Shallow's Star-chamber action, (iii) 'guest-cavalier,' though apparently in apposition to 'my knight,' might equally well be vocative; Shallow is twice addressed as 'cavaliero' above, and he was also the Host's

guest (v. 2. 3. 52). We conclude, therefore, that the F. 'Shal.' at the beginning of Ford's speech denotes the point in the text at which the deer-stealing plot was surrendered for lack of time, the loose thread being tied up to the most handy peg, which was Ford. Cf. p. 99.

193. *Brook* (Q.) F. 'Broome' and so throughout. The jest at 2. 2. 141 proves that the name was Brook, and it has usually been held that the F. alteration was made 'at the instance of some person of the name of Brook living at Windsor.' [1954] Cf. E. K. Chambers, *William Shakespeare*, i. 433, and Alfred Hart in *The Review of English Studies*, 19 (1943), p. 246 (foot).

196. *Ameers* (Hart) F. 'An-heires' Of the many conjectures, Hart's is undoubtedly the best, and we have ventured to adopt it. Cf. 'Cæsar, Keisar, Pheazar' (1. 3. 10).

2. 2.

1. The Q. reads this line in place of 'Why, then the world's mine oyster,' etc. Feeling, as all critics have done, that it is unquestionably Shakespeare's, Theobald followed by Malone and others tacked it on to the end of the 'oyster' speech, thereby making nonsense. It forms, however, a good opening to the scene. v. G. 'equipage.'

5–12. *Not a penny* etc. Cf. pp. 95–6, and 133.

8. *coach-fellow* (F. and Q.) Most edd. explain as 'yoke-fellow' (cf. *Hen. V*. 2. 3. 56). Theobald emended 'couch-fellow,' i.e. Pistol and Nym could not afford a bed apiece, which gives excellent sense. 'Couch' is misprinted 'coach' in *Oth.* 4. 1. 72—an *a*: minim misprint (v. T.I. p. xli).

14–23. *Reason...lurch*. Here, as in ll. 5–12, the Q. is too close to F. in punctuation and spelling to be 'reported' matter, v. pp. 95–6.

20. *honour* F. 'hononer'

20-1. *Ay, ay, I* F. 'I, I, I'—which all edd. follow, except G. White who reads 'I, ay, I'. 'Ay' is always spelt 'I' in F., and Falstaff was given to 'sighing and grief,' when it suited his purpose.

21. *God* (Q.) F. 'heauen', in accordance with the Jacobean blasphemy law.

24. *rags,* F. 'raggs;' Becket suggested 'rages' which gives perhaps better sense.

25. *bold-beating* Unexplained; passage not in Q. We suggest *bowl-beating*. 'Boule' (= bowl) and 'bould' (= bold) are both Shakespearian spellings. The problem, therefore, resolves itself into an *e : d* error, v. T.I. p. xli and cf. *M.N.D.* 5. 1. 336 'beholds' for 'behowls.' 'Bowl-beating (i.e. pot-thumping) oaths' belong to the same family as 'red-lattice phrases'; drinking-bowls were, of course, made of pewter, and Cloten broke a man's pate with one (*Cym.* 2. 1. 5). Hamner suggested 'bull-baiting'.

27. *relent* (F.) Q. 'recant', which may be preferred. *wouldst* (Q.) F. 'would'

34–5. Note the rhyme, confirmed by F. arrangement, which we retain. Falstaff's reply is a line of verse. Possibly fossils from the unrevised play.

50, 54. *God* (Q.) F. 'heauen' v. note l. 21 *supra*.

59. *when the court lay at Windsor* This, in F. brackets, is curious, since Caius goes to court in 1. 4, and Quickly herself later in this speech talks of receiving 'twenty angels' from courtiers 'this morning.' The court *is* at Windsor, as she speaks; it is also legitimate to assume that the court actually 'lay at Windsor' at the time of 'the command performance' of the play. Presumably, then, these words were added to Quickly's part for some occasion when the court was obviously *not* at Windsor, e.g. for the performance at Whitehall in Nov. 1604, v. p. xxi *n*.

63. *gift;* F. 'gift,' *sweetly,* F. 'sweetly;'

102. *Ford's wife,* F. 'Fords wife;'

127–9. *This pink* etc. This strange speech, Pistol's last words in the play *in persona sua*, is we believe a loose thread of a plot never worked out owing to lack of time, but intended to connect *The Merry Wives* with the Prince Hal cycle (cf. note 3. 2. 65 and p. 99). Quickly is, of course, Pistol's 'prize' in *Hen. V*. That Pistol's lines were an 'addition' carelessly introduced into the middle of Falstaff's speech is suggested by 'Sayst thou so' (l. 130) which refers directly to 'This news distracts me' (l. 126) and is most awkwardly separated from it. Cf. Hart, *Introd.* p. lxii.

127. *pink* (Warburton) F. 'puncke'—a minim-error; even Pistol would hardly call his future wife a 'punk.' 'Pink'= (*a*) a fishing-vessel, a good description of Quickly (v. N.E.D., which gives 15th and 16th cent. instances); (*b*) a fashionable beauty, which would also suit here—ironically. The context, wholly nautical, makes Warburton's emendation, we believe, certain.

141. *o'erflow* (Capell) F. 'ore'flows'

168. *a scholar* Cf. note 1. 3. 3. The whole dialogue 'reads like an extract from another play' (cf. note 2. 1. 51–5); it is neither Falstaffian nor Shakespearian, and we regard it as another fossil from the old play.

194–5. *Love like a shadow* etc. F. prints these lines in italics and with inverted commas (v. *To the Reader*, Inverted Commas). See p. 133 for probable source in Horace's *Satires*.

246, 262. *at night* v. pp. xvii–xviii.

284. *effect*, F. 'effect;'

285. *God* (Q.) F. 'Heauen' v. note 2. 2. 21.

2. 3.

3. *de* (F3) F. 'the'

6, 7, 33. *no-come* (F.) The hyphen marks the accent of the Frenchman.

23. *punto* F. 'puncto' v. G.

26. *Galen* F. 'Galien' but spelt correctly at 3. 1. 63.

30. *Castilian-King-Urinal* F. 'Caftalion-king-Vrinall' i.e. Caius is the 'Keisar' of urinals—the urinal of Philip II of Spain, the most powerful monarch 'of de vorld,' who

after a long and painful illness died in 1598. The passage can scarcely have been penned after this date.

52. *guest-justice* This and 'master guest' (l.67) are the only indications in the received text that Shallow was staying at the Garter; but v. note 2. 1. 191.

53. *Mock-water* Q. agrees. 'Muck-water' (Farmer) = liquid manure (cf. 'urinal,' 'stale') is plausible; the primary sense, however, has something to do with 'valour,' which suggests 'Make-water' (Cartwright). Perhaps we should read:

Host. ...a word, Mounseur Muck-water.
Caius. Mock-vater? vat is dat?
Host. Make-water, in our English tongue, is valour, bully.

58. *cut his ears* Referring to 'jack-dog'= mongrel.

81. *Cried-game* Many conjectures, most edd. (except Hart) reading 'Cried I aim?' v. 'cry aim' G. F. reads in full 'and thou ſhalt wooe her: Cride-game, ſaid I well?' Q. (here almost certainly reported) 'And thou ſhalt wear hir cried game: ſed I well bully.' We believe F. gives the true reading. The colon, capital and hyphen suggest that the word is an insult (the Host's parting shot), and the most obvious interpretation is that Caius is the 'game,' after whom the hounds of ridicule are now in full 'cry.' Possibly sporting slang, now lost.

3. 1.

S.D. (i) *two stiles*, etc. v. note l. 26. (ii) *an open book* cf. ll. 37, 41. Shallow takes the book to be a Bible; but Evans' songs suggest that it was some 'Book of Songs and Sonnets,' borrowed perhaps from 'Master Slender's serving-man'—and librarian.

2. *name*, F. 'name;'

5. *pittie-ward* (F.) Much annotated, the favourite reading being 'petty-ward.' N.E.D. gives 'pittie' as 16th cent. sp. of 'petty,' but possibly 'pittie'= Pity, i.e. *pietà*, and was connected with the Church of the

Blessed Virgin in Windsor, which Camden describes.
park-ward, F. 'Parke-ward:'

11. *cholers* F. 'Chollors'—a common 16th cent. sp.

16. *To shallow rivers* etc. Marlowe—a little scratched.
F. prints in prose, but in italics; it would be in Evans'
part, perhaps picked out in 'Italian' script. N.B. Evans'
pointing of the song resembles that of the Prologue in
'Pyramus and Thisbe.'

23. *When as I sat in Pabylon* = first line of Ps. 137
(metrical version).

26. *Yonder he is coming* The context makes it clear
that Caius is meant. The two parties come different ways:
Shallow, etc. over the stile from Windsor (cf. 2. 3. 69);
Caius, etc. along the field-path from Frogmore (cf. 2. 3.
72). Evans stands between the advancing parties, but
does not see Caius at first.

40. *Got-pless* (Walker) F. 'Pleffe' v. note 2. 2. 21.
The words 'from his mercy sake' require 'Got.'

78. *Pray you...good time* i.e. the occasion calls for
patience.

81. *laughing-stogs* (Capell) F. 'laughing-stocks'—but
cf. F. 'vlowting-stog' (l. 111).

84. *urinals* (Q. Capell) F. 'Vrinal'

85. *for missing* etc. All edd. since Pope have adopted
this Q. passage.

99–100. *Give me...terrestrial; so* All edd. since Theobald have adopted this. *celestial;* F. '(celeftiall)'

105. *lads* (Q. Warburton) F. 'Lad'

113. *to be revenge* etc. Hart notes this as the first
hint of the horse-stealing plot. Cf. pp. xix–xxi and note
4. 3. 1–2.

3. 2.

1. *little gallant;* F. '(little Gallant)'
16. *weathercock* v. G. and cf. 1. 3. 83; 3. 3. 24, 31.
31. *twelve score* i.e. yards. Cf. *2 H. IV*, 3. 2. 48, n.

49–51. *And so…speak of* F. prints as verse. Cf. note
2. 1. 17–27.

63. *'tis in his buttons* Many conjectures, none satis-
factory. Read '*'tis in his talons*' and cf. 'a' babbled'
misprinted 'a table' *Hen. V.* 2. 3. 18 (Sir Edward
Maunde Thompson: privately). 'He will carry't' suggests hawking; to 'carry' meaning to fly away with the
game or quarry. Q. reads 'betmes'

65. *the wild Prince and Poins* v. p. 99. The only direct
link in the F. with *Hen. IV*; but cf. notes 2. 2. 127–9;
5. 5. 99, S.D.

80. *drink in pipe-wine…dance* An elaborate quibble
on the Host's 'canary,' which means both a dance and
a wine. 'Pipe'= (*a*) a large cask; hence 'pipe-wine'
= wine from the wood. N.B. Falstaff, the 'tun of man,'
might be called a 'pipe' and his cries 'whine'; (*b*) a
musical instrument for a dance; hence 'pipe-wine'= the
whine of the pipe. 'Drink in'= listen to, or watch with
delight.

3. 3.

3. *Robin* i.e. apparently Robert, the servant, not the
page.

13. *Datchet-mead* F.'Dotchet Mead'; *a*:*o* misprint—
spelt correctly later.

24. *Jack-a-lent* v. G. Cf. 1. 3. 83; 3. 2. 16. It is clear
from Mrs Page's next speech that Robin's gaudy clothes
were in need of repair.

40. *Have I caught* etc. (Q.) F. 'Haue I caught thee,
my heauenly Iewel?' The line is from Sidney's *Astrophel
and Stella* (1591), and Q. quotes correctly. Note the date.

52. *arched beauty* Q. 'arched bent'—which may be
preferred.

57. *Thou art a tyrant* Q. 'By the Lord, thou art a
traitor'—which most edd. read. But F. 'tyrant' is an obvious quibble upon 'tire.' 'Thou art too cruel to thyself'
is the meaning.

60. *if fortune thy foe* etc. (F2) F. 'if Fortune thy foe, were not Nature thy friend.' Possibly we should read 'if fortune, thy foe, were but as nature, thy friend'— which gives the required sense.

65. *persuade thee there's* (Q.) F.'perſwade thee. Ther's' N.B. Q's exact reading is 'perſwade thee/Ther's'— 'Ther's' beginning a new line, since the speech is printed in short lengths, suggestive of player's part (cf. note 2. 1. 17–27). This perhaps explains the F. error, that text being also we believe derived from players' parts. Cf. similar error noted under 2. 1. 140.

81. S.D. *Robin enters* Most edd. read 'Robin [within].' The F. does not help us, of course; v. p. 93.

103. *house—* F. 'houſe;'

131. S.D. *in his ear* Q. reads 'Aſide'

145. *who goes here?* Q. reading required by l. 170 below, and 3. 5. 94.

150–2. *Buck?* etc. F. prints these three lines as verse. N.B. 'and of the season too it shall appear' *is* a line of verse. Cf. note 2. 1. 121–2.

152. *season too* F. 'ſeaſon too;'

172. *have need of washing* i.e. because he will have 'berayed himself' with fright.

183. *foolish carrion* (F2) F. 'fooliſhion Carion'

191. *Heard you that?* To this Q. adds 'Miſ. For. I, I, peace.'

214. *walk in the Park* i.e. take a turn till dinner is ready. Edd. have not realised that a dinner in Ford's house follows this, and have thus failed to understand what happens in the next scene. Page's 'Let's go in' (l. 218) means, we take it, 'Let's accept the invitation.' They were, of course, standing in the hall (i.e. on the outer-stage), not the dining-chamber, so that 'in' is quite appropriate.

220. *breakfast* An early one, as hawking began at sunrise; v. Dover Wilson, *Life in Shakespeare's England*, p. 276.

224. *If there be one or two* etc. Q., which misplaces this, gives Evans the retort 'In your teeth for shame.'

226–7. *remembrance...mine host* Another relic of the horse-stealing plot, v. note 4. 3. 1–2.

3. 4.

S.D. Capell, followed by all edd., heads this scene 'A room in Page's house.' But (i) had Fenton been indoors when Page arrived he would surely have been asked to leave; instead he is allowed to remain until the end of the scene; (ii) Page bids Shallow and Slender 'come in' (l. 76), while Mrs Page says that Anne 'must needs go in' (l. 93). From all this it is clear that the scene takes place *outside* Page's house; and once the place is determined the *time* which has puzzled all (v. Daniel, p. 127) is also explained. At 3. 2. 50 we learn that Shallow and Slender are 'to dine with Mistress Anne' (N.B. not 'with Mistress Page'); a few lines later, Page accepts Ford's invitation to dinner, upon which Shallow comments 'we shall have the freer wooing at Master Page's'; Mrs Page is, of course, already at Ford's house; and, as we have seen (v. note 3. 3. 214) Mr and Mrs Page dine with the Fords, returning home in the present scene, after dinner. It follows that 3. 4. opens immediately after, or towards the end of the Shallow-Slender dinner 'with Mistress Anne.' We are not told how Fenton comes to be there; but Quickly's presence makes us suspect that she arrives with Fenton, fetches Anne out to him, and remains behind to keep Shallow and Slender in play, until, their patience exhausted, they sally forth to find their hostess dallying with Fenton.

1–2. *I see I cannot* etc. Q. begins this scene with ten lines, divided between Fenton and Anne, which form a natural introduction to the F. opening. We conclude that this dialogue was 'cut' in revision, v. pp. 99–100.

12. F. omits the prefix *Fen.* to this speech.

21. *why then hark you hither!* Most edd. read 'why, then,—hark you hither! [*they converse apart.*' But there are no stops in F. and it seems more natural to take Anne as meaning 'if all else fails come back to me.'

47. *under the degree of a squire* Under = in the condition of (Hart). v. G. 'cut and long-tail.'

69. *Fenton* F. 'Fenter'

89. *Fenton* F. prints this with l. 90.

104. *Mistress Anne;* F. 'Miſtris Anne,'

109. *another errand to Sir John Falstaff* etc. (i) there has been no opportunity for Quickly to hear of this errand, (ii) 'what a beast am I to slack it' suggests that she hurries off to the Garter Inn forthwith, whereas she does not really arrive until next morning (3. 5). We believe that the passage may be a piece of actor's gag. Cf. p. xvii.

3. 5.

4–17. *Have I lived…mummy* The punctuation of this speech in Q. is practically identical with that of F. (v. pp. 95–6). N.B. It is Falstaff's 'part,' like 2. 2. 5–12.

9. *slighted* Perhaps we should read 'sleighted' i.e. 'conveyed dexterously,' with a quibble upon 'slided,' which Q. reads.

30. *sperm* F. 'Sperſme'

73, 80. *wife's* F. 'wiues' N.B. Q. agrees.

83. *By the Lord,* (Q.) F. 'Yes'

110–11. (*in that surge!*) F. 'in that serge'

136. *avoid,* F. 'auoid:'

4. 1.

14. *accidence* William's catechism is based upon the first few pages of Lilly's 'Latin Grammar.'

46. *O! vocativo*—O. Possibly the second 'O' should be 'ho,' i.e. William's shot for the vocative of 'hic.'

61. *lunatics* (Capell) F. 'Lunaties'

4. 2.

4. *accoutrement* (Capell) F. 'accuſtrement'—a 16th cent. form.

20. *lunes* (Theobald) F. 'lines' Cf. *Wint.* 2. 2. 30 'Lunes'; *Troil.* 2. 3. 139 'lines.' Henry Bradley (Sh. Eng. ii. 572) writes 'The Warwickshire "on a line," meaning "in a rage," supplies justification for the F. reading "lines" in two of these cases.' But 'lune' (= a fit of lunacy) has etymological support (v. N.E.D. 'lune' 2), and the *Troil.* passage is clearly astrological in reference, suggesting 'lunes'= moons. Further, 'lune' had two other meanings both significant in the present connexion: (i) a leash for a hawk. N.E.D. quotes 'In fancy's lunes I fast was caught' (Gifford, 1580), where the play upon 'lunes' (madness) is palpable; (ii) astrological figures. Cf. l. 210 below 'scrape the figures out of your husband's brains,' where Mrs Page still has 'lunes' in mind. Finally Ford's distemper is not 'anger' or 'rage' but 'madness' (cf. ll. 117–19). With most edd. we believe Theobald to be right. If so, F. 'lines' is a simple minim-misprint.

husband; F. 'huſband,'

23. *forehead,* F. 'for-head:'

30. *here;* F. 'heere,'

52. *Mistress Page* (Malone) F. '*Miſt. Ford.*' It is impossible that this and the speech beginning l. 55 can both be spoken by the same character, v. next note.

60. *Mistress Page* (Malone) F. '*Miſt. Ford*'—thus giving two consecutive speeches to the same character. This supports the alteration at l. 52. But v. p. 134.

96. *misuse him enough* (F2) F. 'miſuſe enough'

100. *Still swine* etc. v. G.

107. *as lief* (F2) F. 'liefe as'

113. *ging* (F2) F. 'gin'—a variant 16th cent. sp., v. G.

114. *the devil be shamed* i.e. by the truth.

135. *I shall find you* v. G. 'find you.'

136. *wife's* F. 'wiues' Q. agrees.

150. *you must pray* Cf. 3. 3. 205. Evans, like Page, supposes that Ford must be under the influence of evil spirits. Cf. Lavater, *Of Ghostes and Spirits* (1572), p. 193, 'It behoueth them that are vexed with spirites, to pray especially.'

158. *leman* with a quibble on 'lemon.'

167. *comes of errands* Ford suspects Mrs Prat to be a go-between.

175. *let him not strike* (F2) F. 'let him ſtrike'

178. *I'll prat her* v. G. 'prat.'

179. *rag* Most edd. emend to 'hag,' v. G.

180. *ronyon* F. 'Runnion'

192. *open* v. G.

205. *in fee-simple* v. G. 'fee-simple.'

217. *with it! then shape it:* F. 'with it, then ſhape it:'

4. 3.

1–2. *the Germans...the duke* This scene, 4. 5. 59–84, and 4. 6. 1–5, together with a few loose threads (e.g. 2. 1. 88; 3. 1. 113; 3. 3. 226–9; 5. 5. 110–11), are all that are left in the received text of the Mümpellgart horse-stealing plot (v. Introd. pp. xix–xxi and p. 98). To Hart belongs the credit of reconstructing the lost story from these scattered hints (v. his *Introd.* pp. lxxii–lxxvii). Briefly, Evans and Caius revenge themselves upon the Host by engaging Pistol, Nym and Rugby to impersonate Germans in the service of Count Garmomble, to demand three of the Host's horses in his name, and then to run off with them. We have only to add that it looks as if Ford, possibly with Shallow as accomplice, arranged that the loss should fall upon Falstaff, whose horses were 'arrested' (5. 5. 111), the Host doubtless being allowed to hold them in pawn until such time (which would never come) as the knight could repay Ford his twenty pounds.

1. *the Germans desire* (Capell) F. 'the Germane defires' Cf. note l. 7.

4. *What duke should that be* etc. This contradicts l. 9 which makes it clear that the Host was expecting the Duke as his guest. We suggest that this speech, which tallies closely with 4. 5. 81 (v. note), was inserted during revision in order to cover up the Mümpellgart traces.

7. *Ay, sir;* F. 'I Sir?' *them* (Q.) F. 'him' It is noteworthy that in F. Bardolph speaks of one 'German' but the Host of 'Germans' (cf. l. 1). Perhaps Bardolph's part was carelessly copied. *I'll call them to you.* This suggests that the original scene may have been longer and included dialogue between the Host and 'the Germans.'

9. *house* (Q.) F. 'howfes'

4. 4.

S.D. We left Shallow and Caius at Ford's house in 4. 2. Neither reappears here. Cf. note 5. 2. 8 and pp. 99–100. This scene bears all the marks of hasty revision. N.B. prose and verse mixed throughout; but method in it, e.g. (i) ll. 1–5 look like an introductory prose-patch to take the place of lengthier verse-dialogue (cf. note 4. 6. 1); (ii) after this, except for ll. 18–19, all the prose in the scene belongs to Evans, whose part, if originally in verse (and there are traces of this), would naturally have to be revised.

1. *pest* F. 'beft' Cf. note 1. 1. 38.

7. *cold* (Rowe) F. 'gold'—surely an error of dictation?

8. *Than...stand* This long line perhaps represents two verse-fragments of the original spliced together.

11–12. *Be not...offence* F. prints as one line. N.B. 'As in offence'= broken line, suggesting abridgment.

18–19. *How?...never come.* Capell omitted 'to' and read as two lines of verse. We suggest that 'To send... Park/At midnight...he will never come' represent two lines from the end of a longer speech in the original, and that the reviser added 'How?' to link it up with Ford's speech.

20–24. Note that 'You say he has been thrown in[to] the river' would make a line of verse; a supposition which finds support in the colon which F. reads after 'rivers.' Further Page's 'So think I too' looks like a scrap of verse.

28–29. *There is...forest* F. divides 'There is...Herne the Hunter...Forreſt' which suggests revision.

28. *Herne the hunter* F. gives 'Herne', Q. 'Horne' throughout. We suggest that Q. is correct here, as in 'Brook' (v. note 2. 1. 193). The name 'Horn' would account for the legend, while the Q. line, which we adopt at l. 43, 'Disguised like Horne, with huge horns on his head' stresses the name with a quibble. Halliwell traced a 'Rycharde Horne, yeoman' who poached the king's forests in Henry VIII's reign (v. Hart, *Introd.* p. li).

43. *Disguised like Herne* etc. Q. reads 'Horne' here (v. previous note). The line is necessary to the sense, since Page's 'And in this shape' (l. 45) requires it, and F. nowhere explicitly states that Falstaff's assumption of the 'Herne' rôle is a part of the plot.

44. *let it not be doubted* etc. Page's doubts (cf. l. 18) have been laid to rest; but we are not told how, probably because Mrs Ford's explanation (? following l. 43) has been 'cut.' It is clear, however, that Mrs Quickly is armed with weighty arguments, but she fires them off in Falstaff's 'chamber,' so that we never hear them.

47. *upon,* F. 'vpon:' 64. *dis-horn* etc. Cf. p. 134.

68. *jack-an-apes* v. G. and cf. notes 5. 3. 11; 5. 4. S.D.; 5. 5. 133, 157–8.

70. *That...vizards* F. arranges as two half-lines.

71–2. *My Nan...white* F. arranges as prose.

73. *time* Theobald suggests 'tire' (i.e. a minim-error), which makes better sense.

75. *And marry* etc. This long line is suspicious; perhaps 'Go, send to Falstaff straight' is the reviser's addition to a broken line. Cf. note l. 83.

80. *Let us about it* F. prints this as second half of l. 79, which suggests that Evans spoke verse in a previous existence.

82. broken line, significantly following a speech by Evans.

83. *Send Quickly* (Theobald) F. 'Send quickly' Quickly goes, of course, in 4. 5. It is curious that *two* messengers should be sent. As Brook's last interview is not found in Q., that and Ford's speech, ll. 76-7, may have been inserted by the revisers. Cf. note l. 75.

4. 5.

1-2. Hart suggests that the Host's haste is prompted by his preoccupation with the impending visit of the Duke.

6. *his castle* Greg believes this to be an allusion to Oldcastle; cf. 1 *Hen. IV*, 1. 2. 47, 'My old lad of the castle' and v. note 1. 3. 3. Robertson (pp. 27–30) supports this and points out that where 'Falstaff' stands in the Q. verse, the lines are generally a syllable short.

28. *sir, Master* (Steevens) F. '(Sir) my mafter'

40. *I may not conceal* etc. F. gives this to Falstaff; Rowe corrects.

50. *Ay, Sir Tyke; who more bold?* (Farmer, followed by Malone and many mod. edd.) F. 'I Sir: like who more bold.' Q. 'I tike, who more bold.' Q., though probably 'reported' here, almost certainly preserves the original sense, the F. reading being both pointless and obscure. N.B. Falstaff clearly makes a 'hit,' since the Host congratulates him upon it when Simple goes out. A tyke was, of course, not 'bold'; while Falstaff may also be quibbling upon Simple's 'say so,' taking it as ''say soe,' i.e. try the refuse-bin, which is what a tyke would do (v. N.E.D. 'say' = to try by tasting, and 'soe' = tub). The reading

also gives point to 'mussel-shell' (v. G.); Simple had evidently a dog-face.

53. *Thou art clerkly* F. 'Thou are clearkly' For 'clerkly,' cf. note 1. 3. 3. N.E.D. quotes from a chemical writer of 1594 a sentence which reads curiously like a comment upon this passage: 'Not any one of them hath so clarkly wrought vpon this simple...as to hide the taste.'

59–84. *Out, alas, sir!* etc. Cf. note 4. 3. 1–2 and pp. xix–xxi.

65–6. *They are gone* etc. This speech is not in Q.; possibly added in revision to soften down the Mümpell-gart reference. N.B. 'Germans are honest men.' Cf. notes 4. 3. 4, and l. 81 below.

71. *cozen-germans* F. 'Cozen-Iermans' i.e. false Germans. Q. 'cofen garmombles' i.e. cousin-Mombell-gards, v. pp. xix–xxi and note 4. 3. 1–2. There are other points about this speech in Q. which show that it derives from a different version than that in F. Evans' parting shot is 'grate why mine Hoft,' and 'grate why,' as Hart has shown, is a corruption of the Welsh 'cadw chwi' (i.e. 'bless you'; v. Nares, 'Du cata whee'), which as 'gat a whee,' 'cat a whee,' or 'cata-why' is not uncommon in Eliz. literature. 'grate' is probably a misprint or transcriber's error for 'gate' or 'gata.'

74. *vlouting-stogs* (Capell) F. 'vlouting-ftocks' Cf. note 3. 1. 81.

80. *duke de Jarmany* F. 'Duke de Iamanie' We take 'Iamanie' to be a minim-error for 'Iarmanie,' a common 16th cent. sp. of 'Germany' (cf. F. 'Iermans,' l. 71), which occurs in the 'Shakespearian' Addition to *Sir Thomas More* (v. T.I. p. xxix). We probably, therefore, ought to read 'Germany' here in a modernised text.

81. *dere is no duke* etc. As the Caius incursion, unlike that of Evans, is patently 'reported' in the Q., it follows that it did not exist in the text upon which the pirate worked; and this implicit disavowal of any connexion

with Mümpellgart was, we suspect, inserted by the revisers. Cf. notes 4. 3. 4; ll. 65–6 above.

94. *to say my prayers* All edd. since Pope have adopted
these words.

4. 6.

1. *Master Fenton* etc. This prose line, the only prose
in the scene except 6–7, suggests adaptation in order to
shorten a lengthier opening (cf. note 4. 4. S.D.), more
especially as ll. 1 and 2 are printed together as prose in F.

6. *Master Fenton;* F. '(Mafter Fenton)'

16–17. *fat Falstaff|Hath a great scene* Q. 'Wherein fat
Falstaffe had a mightie fcare' An interesting link between
F. and Q. is to be observed here. Note (i) that if the F.
passage be omitted, verse and sense are improved, (ii) that
precisely the same is true of the Q. line, which thus
appears in its context:

> And in a robe of white this night difguifed,
> Wherein fat *Falstaffe* had a mightie fcare,
> Muft *Slender* take her and carrie her to *Catlen,*
> And there vnknowne to any, marrie her.

The reference to Falstaff is obviously a hasty addition in
both texts. Cf. Robertson, p. 29.

26. *Now, sir* F. prints this with l. 25; possibly patch-
work to cover a rent.

27. *ever* (Pope) F. 'euen'—a minim-error.

39. *denote* (Capell) F. 'deuote'

5. 1.

8. *mince* v. G.

12. *yesterday* Ford should, of course, say 'this
morning.' Daniel makes much of the time-confusion in
this play; but with our arrangement of the scenes (cf. note
3. 4. S.D.) Ford's 'yesterday' is the only really serious
error in the text. Cf. Introd. p. xviii.

5. 2.

3. *daughter* F. omits.

6. *mum...budget* v. G.

8. *Shallow* Note that he does not appear in 5. 5. Cf. 4. 4. S.D. and p. 99. The Q. gives him an entry and one short speech in the last scene; the F. leaves him in the castle-ditch.

10. *ten o'clock* The rendezvous was for ''twixt twelve and one' (v. 4. 6. 19). Two hours and a bit was a long time for old Justice Shallow to lie 'couched i'th' castle-ditch'! Possibly 'ten' is an error for 'twelve.'

11. *light and spirits* Probably we should read 'light and sprite' or 'lights and sprites.' Cf. *Troil.* 5. 1. 74 'Hey-day! Spirits and fires.'

5. 3.

11. *the Welsh devil-hern* F. 'the Welch-deuill Herne' Capell reads 'Hugh' for 'Herne,' and most edd. follow him. The F. is vindicated, when we understand Evans' costume. He is to be a 'jack-an-apes' (4. 4. 68), Falstaff calls him a 'Welsh goat' (5. 5. 133) and 'the Welsh flannel' (5. 5. 157), while Q. gives S.D. for 5. 5. 37, 'Enter fir Hugh like a Satyre' etc. Now a satyr was a kind of devil, for the Elizabethans, and Evans, no doubt, wore the appropriate horned-mask. Thus he was a 'devil-hern' in two senses: (i) 'hern' or 'harn'= brain; here used of the head, v. N.E.D. 'harn,' (ii) his function was to 'devil' Herne-Falstaff.

17, 18. *mocked* v. G.

5. 4.

We are tempted to place this scene before 5. 3., where from ll. 10–13 it is clear that the Fairies have preceded the merry wives into the Park. Being only a single speech of three and a half lines it was very liable to get misplaced in 'part'-copy. On the other hand, it forms an effective climax in its present position.

S.D. *Sir Hugh...horns* v. notes 5. 3. 11; 5. 5. 133.
Pistol attired as Puck At 5. 5. 42, 83, 88, F. reads '*Piſt.*'
Possibly Pistol's appearance was simply due to the
exigencies of the cast and had no dramatic significance,
i.e. the audience were not intended to recognise him.
But as his revenge would be fed by Falstaff's exposure,
we have given him an entry. *Quickly in white* etc.
Q. names Quickly 'like the Queene of Fayries' in S.D.
for 5. 5. 37, and F. and Q. head the Fairy-Queen's
speeches 'Qui' and 'Quic' respectively. The boy, therefore, who played Quickly also played the Fairy-Queen.
Is it anything more than a case of 'doubling,' or are we
to suppose that Fenton's gold had won Quickly over to
take the part which Slender supposed to be Anne's?
In this connexion, it must be remembered that Slender
discovers the Fairy-Queen to be 'a great lubberly boy.'
This, however, is not entirely conclusive, since the
audience would know that Quickly was played by a boy,
and their knowledge of this might have been utilised to
enhance the comic effect of Slender's discomfiture.
Anne Page We are not told her colour; but grey would
suit her. *William* v. 4. 4. 48. *red* v. note 5. 5. 99.
many other boys cf. 'twenty glow-worms' (5. 5. 78).

1. *come;* F. 'Come,'
2. *I pray you;* F. '(I pray you)' *pit;* F. 'pit,'

5. 5.

2. *the hot-blooded gods* etc. The Falstaff of *M.W.W.* is
learned to the last; cf. note 1. 3. 3.

14. *tallow* v. G.

24. *a bribed-buck* Theobald reads 'bribe-buck' and
most edd. follow. 'Bribe' originally meant 'to steal'
(v. N.E.D.). 'A bribed-buck,' therefore, is a stolen deer,
which the poachers hurriedly cut up after bringing it
down (cf. Sh. Eng. ii. 345) so as to bear it, if necessary,
'cleanly by the keeper's nose' (*Tit.* 2. 1. 94).

25. *fellow of this walk* v. G.

27. *a woodman* Cf. *Meas.* 4. 3. 170.

34–5. *I think the devil* etc. We preserve F. arrange-ment, since these lines seem to be intended as verse—possibly relics of the old play.

37–105. v. p. 94. At the beginning of this verse-dialogue stands the only internal entry in the F. text, i.e. 'Enter Fairies.' This fact, taken in conjunction with ll. 56–73 which were almost certainly composed for the 'command performance,' suggests that we have here a passage, written out possibly on a separate sheet of foolscap, by one of the revisers, who followed the old text so closely or was so ignorant of the spirit of the rest of the play that he commits the error of placing verse in the mouth of Falstaff. N.B. also the speeches of Evans (the Satyr) show no trace of 'Welsh' in this section.

37. S.D. Cf. 4. 4. 50–55 'Like urchins…diffuséd song.' Q. reads: '*Enter fir Hugh like a Satyre, and boyes dreft like Fayries, mistreffe Quickly, like the Queene of Fayries: they fing a fong about him, and afterwards fpeake*'; v. 5. 4. S.D.

39. *orphan* Theobald reads 'ouphen,' which makes good sense and is palaeographically plausible. Cf. l. 57 and 4. 4. 50 'ouphs.' If Theobald be right, *heirs of fixéd destiny* means, we take it, that they were condemned to the night; cf. l. 38 and *M.N.D.* 4. 1. 97–102. But 'orphan' is possible and may refer to the popular super-stition connecting fairies with the souls of dead children; which finds expression in Vergil (*Aen.* vi. 426–9).

42. *Puck* v. note 5. 4. S.D. For 'Crier Hobgoblin' (l. 41) Q. reads 'Puck'

51. *Raise up the organs* etc. 'Give her elevating and pleasant dreams' (Hart).

56–73. *Search Windsor Castle* etc. v. note ll. 37–105. E. K. Chambers (Sh. Eng. i. 100) suggests that these lines were written for a performance at a Garter Feast at Windsor Castle.

62. *balm*, F. 'Balme;'   *flower:* F. 'flowre,'

67. *bears,* F. 'beares:'

70. *emerald tufts* F. 'Emrold-tuffes'

80. *middle earth* v. G.

81–2. *Heavens defend* etc. We arrange as in F.; the lines seem to be intended as verse. Cf. note ll. 37–105.

82. *a piece of cheese* v. G. 'cheese.' Evans smells Falstaff (l. 80); if he takes him for cheese, he will devour him.

84. *trial-fire* v. G.

88. *wood* Cf. note l. 104.

99. S.D. based upon Q., which reads: '*Here they pinch him, and sing about him, & the Doctor comes one way & steales away a boy in red. And Slender another way he takes a boy in greene: And Fenton steals misteris Anne, being in white. And a noyse of hunting is made within: and all the Fairies runne away. Falstaffe pulles of his bucks head, and rises vp. And enters* M. *Page,* M. *Ford, and their wiues,* M. *Shallow, Sir Hugh.*' N.B. the Q. follows this with a speech by Falstaff in which occur the words 'What hunting at this time of night? Ile lay my life the mad Prince of Wales is stealing his fathers Deare,' cf. note 3. 2. 65.

100. *watched* v. G.

104. *fair yokes* i.e. the horns. Mrs Page, of course, has cuckoldry in mind and is talking 'at' Ford. Hart suggests a quibble upon 'oaks'; the horns appear to have been fashioned from oak-boughs; cf. l. 88.

111. *his horses are arrested* Cf. notes 2. 1. 88; 4. 3. 1–2.

113. *mate* F. 'meete' The emendation seems self-evident; they had 'met' three times, but never 'mated.' 'Meat' was a common 16th cent. sp. of 'mate' (cf. *Two Gent.* note 1. 2. 69 and v. N.E.D.), and Wyld (*Hist. of Mod. Colloquial English,* p. 210) shows that the two words were pronounced alike as late as 1685.

116. *ox* v. G.

117–23. *And these are not fairies* etc. This language

is so extraordinary for Falstaff, in any mood, that the passage must be a relic of the old play. Cf. notes 2. 1. 51–5; 2. 2. 168 and pp. xxiv–xxv.

133. *a Welsh goat* i.e. the Welsh Satyr (cf. note 5. 3. 11).

134. *frieze* A cloth of Welsh manufacture, which no doubt Evans wore as part of his Satyr-costume.

136. *pelly* (F2) F. 'belly'

147. *flax* 'A bag of flax,' though paralleled by 'wool-sack' (1 *Hen. IV*, 2. 4. 148), seems pointless after 'hodge-pudding' (v. G.). We suggest *flux* (v. G. 'flax' and cf. 1 *Hen. IV*, 2. 4. 495–8)—an *a: u* misprint, v. T.I. p. xli.

155. *starings* v. G.

157–8. *Welsh flannel* A reference to Evans' Satyr-costume; v. note 5. 3. 11.

158. *plummet* Many, unnecessary, attempts to emend this; a quibble on 'flannel,' v. G. 'plummet.'

169. *Doctors doubt that* Printed as a separate line in F., and almost certainly intended for Page's ear—the time-honoured jest concerning doubts on paternity.

179. *swinged* A quibble, v. G.

190. *white* F. 'greene'—194. *green* F. 'white'—200. *green* F. 'white': careless transposition, which Pope first rectified.

198. *un garçon...un paysan* F. 'oon Garſon...oon peſant' Cf. note 1. 4. 42.

201. *by gar...by gar* F. 'bee gar...be gar' N.B. 'begar' is the Q. form.

225. *a special stand* v. G. 'stand.'

Additional Notes, 1954

2. 2. 1–5. Professor Alexander (*Edinburgh Bib. Soc. Trans.* II, Pt. 4. pp. 411–13; and *The Tudor Shakespeare* ad loc.) reads plausibly:

Fal. I will not lend thee a penny.
Pist. I will retort the sum in equipage.
Fal. Not a penny.
Pist. Why then...etc.

2. 2. 194–5. Probably a reflexion of Horace, *Sat.* I, ii, 108:

> Meus est amor huic similis; nam
> Transvolat in media posita, et fugientia captat.

And perhaps suggested by Montaigne's comment upon this (*Essays* ii, ch. xv. Florio's trans.): 'Our appetite doth contemne and passe over what he hath in his free choice and owne possession, to runne after and pursue what he hath not

> It over flies what open lies,
> Pursuing onely that which flies.'

4. 2. 52, 60. Sir Walter Greg conjectured (private letter dated 17 January 1922) that these speeches should be divided thus:

Mistress Ford. There they always use to discharge their birding-pieces.
Mistress Page. Creep into the kiln-hole.

and

Mistress Ford. If you go out in your own semblance, you die, Sir John.
Mistress Page. Unless you go disguised.

He adds: 'I suggest that in both instances a speaker's name (Mrs P.) has dropt out. Observe that in both cases the first part of the speech would probably fill one line of MS, so that the second half began a fresh line. Either the scribe may have omitted to insert the name or the printer may have overlooked it.'

These redistributions add such point and gaiety to the dialogue that I do not doubt their correctness. Malone conjectured, and Dyce, Craig, Alexander and Sisson have accepted, the earlier one (ll. 52–3).

4. 4. 64. *dis-horn the spirit* In the same letter Greg writes: 'This to my mind is conclusive that the name should be Horne not Herne. There would be little point in saying "take off his horns"—it must mean "strip him of his Horne disguise".'

THE STAGE-HISTORY OF
THE MERRY WIVES OF WINDSOR

The Merry Wives of Windsor has always been popular
in the theatre. The quarto edition of 1602 states that
it had already 'bene diuers times Acted by the right
Honorable my Lord Chamberlaines seruants. Both before her Maiestie, and else-where.' The Revels Accounts
show that it was acted at Whitehall on the Sunday
following Hallowmas Day (i.e. on November 1), 1604.
An old MS printed in George R. Wright's *Archaeologic
and Historic Fragments*, 1887, informs us that 'the mery
wifes of Winsor' was acted before Charles I and Henrietta
Maria by the Lady Elizabeth's servants (the Queen of
Bohemia's Players) at the Cockpit on November 15, 1638.
Pepys saw it at 'the new Theatre' (Killigrew's theatre)
on December 5, 1660, when he liked the humours of
the country gentleman (Slender, possibly acted by Win-
tershal) and the French doctor, but found 'the rest but
very poorly, and Sir J. Falstaffe [Cartwright] as bad as
any'; again at the King's house on September 25, 1661,
when he found it 'ill done'—perhaps because he went
'much against my nature and will, yet such is the power
of the Devil over me I could not refuse it'; and a third
time, at the King's house, on August 15, 1667, when
'it did not please me at all, in no part of it.' Downes, in
his *Roscius Anglicanus*, includes this play among those
which the King's Company acted 'but now and then,'
not among their principal stock plays.

The comedy was not much mauled by revisers. In
1702 John Dennis's 'improved' version of it, *The Comical
Gallant, or the Amours of Sir John Falstaffe*, was put on

at Drury Lane; but it met with little favour, and Dennis complained that his Falstaff (probably Powell) acted badly. In this version Ford, whose assumed name is Broom, not Brook (this error had crept into the prompt-book before 1623), is cured of his jealousy by being beaten by Mistress Page, disguised as a man and purporting to be a lover of Mistress Ford, and beaten again by fairies in the last act, when he is disguised as Falstaff. The stage quickly returned to the original play. Downes (*Roscius Anglicanus*) states that the comedy was acted at the Court of St James's by royal command on April 23, the anniversary of Queen Anne's coronation. He does not give the year, but it must have been 1704, 1705 or 1706. The players were the actors of both houses, with Betterton as Falstaff, Mrs Bracegirdle as Mistress Ford, and Mrs Barry as Mistress Page. Quin played Falstaff at Lincoln's Inn Fields on Oct. 22, 1720, with so much success that the play was given eighteen times that season; and again at Drury Lane, five times successively, in December, 1734. Among other actors who played Falstaff in the eighteenth century were Delane, Stephens, Love, Berry and Shuter, the last being also much liked as Shallow and Slender. At the Haymarket on September 3, 1777, Henderson (who was especially good as the Falstaff of *King Henry IV*) first appeared as the Falstaff of *The Merry Wives of Windsor* and the crowd was so great that 'two audiences went away'—i.e. the house could have been filled three times over. Later we find Lee Lewes, Ryder, Palmer and Fawcett playing Falstaff. Eighteenth century records also show us Mrs Woffington, Mrs Pritchard, Miss Farren and Mrs Pope acting Mistress Ford, while Mrs Pope was frequently seen also as Mistress Page.

In the nineteenth century the popularity of the play did not diminish. In 1804 Cooke played Falstaff at Covent Garden, with John Philip Kemble as Master Ford; and in October, 1816, at Drury Lane, Stephen Kemble made appearances as the Falstaff of *King*

Henry IV and the Falstaff of *The Merry Wives of Windsor*, which called forth one of Hazlitt's shrewdest critical attacks. 'We see no more reason,' he wrote, 'why Mr Stephen Kemble should play Falstaff than why Louis XVIII is qualified to fill a throne, because he is fat, and belongs to a particular family. Every fat man cannot represent a great man.' In February, 1824, Elliston produced at Drury Lane Shakespeare's play turned into an opera by Frederic Reynolds, with added dialogue and 'song cues' and music arranged by Henry Bishop. With Mme Vestris, Miss Stephens and Braham in the cast, the piece was liked, and Mme Vestris appeared in it for her own benefit, at the Haymarket in the October of the same year. This is the last that was heard of Reynolds's opera; though in 1839, when Charles Mathews and Mme Vestris produced the play at Covent Garden, some of Bishop's music still clung to it. In 1851 J. H. Hackett played Falstaff with success under Webster's management at the Haymarket; and Webster himself played Falstaff at the Adelphi in 1853. In November, 1851, Charles Kean at last restored to the stage Shakespeare's play unadulterated. He chose it for the opening of the first season of his sole management at the Princess's Theatre, when Bartley played Falstaff and Harley was excellent as Dr Caius, Mr and Mrs Kean playing the Fords, and Mrs Keeley Mistress Page. The next notable performance of *The Merry Wives of Windsor* was not without addition by another hand. When Samuel Phelps produced the play at the Gaiety Theatre in December, 1874 (having previously acted it at Sadler's Wells), in place of the song, 'Fie on sinful fantasy,' the Anne Page sang (to music by Arthur Sullivan) a song, 'Love laid his sleepless head On a thorny rosy bed,' written for this production by Swinburne and afterwards printed in the Second Series of *Poems and Ballads*. The change incurred, as Dutton Cook recorded, 'the decided displeasure of the audience.' But the performance as a whole was much admired, as it should have been with Phelps as Falstaff, Arthur Cecil as Dr Caius, Hermann Vezin as Master Ford, Johnston Forbes-Robertson as Fenton, Mrs John Wood as Mistress Page, Rose Leclerq as Mistress Ford and Miss Furtado as Anne Page. Herbert Beerbohm Tree's revivals of *The Merry Wives of Windsor* at His Majesty's Theatre, with himself as Falstaff, Miss Ellen Terry as Mistress Ford and Mrs Kendal or Lady Tree as Mistress Page, are within the memory of most living playgoers; and the comedy has been a regular feature of the Benson repertory and a safe attraction at Shakespeare Festivals at Stratford-upon-Avon.

1921   HAROLD CHILD.

GLOSSARY

Note. Where a pun or quibble is intended, the meanings are distinguished as (*a*) and (*b*)

ACTÆON, transformed to a stag with horns and pursued by his own hounds—the classical prototype of the Elizabethan cuckold; 2. 1. 108; 3. 2. 39

ADDITIONS, titles; 2. 2. 275

AGAINST THE HAIR, i.e. against the grain—phrase derived from stroking an animal the wrong way; 2. 3. 36

AGGRAVATE HIS STYLE, i.e. give him a new title, raise him from 'knave' to 'cuckold'; 2. 2. 262

ALLHALLOWMAS, i.e. November 1st. Note that Simple is simple as regards the calendar; 1. 1. 190

ALLICHOLY, blunder for 'melancholy' (cf. *Two Gent.* 4. 2. 26); 1. 4. 148

AMAIMON, a mighty devil; cf. 1 *Hen. IV*, 2. 4. 370 and Scot, *Discoverie of Witchcraft* (ch. 29) 'king Baell or Amoimon'; 2. 2. 274

ANCHOR, 'the anchor is deep'; 1. 3. 50. If not corrupt (v. note), 'anchor' may have parallels in 'my invention...anchors on Isabel,' *Meas.* 2. 4. 3 and *Cym.* 5. 5. 393

ANTHROPOPHAGINIAN, man-eater; 4. 5. 8

ARMIGERO, i.e. 'armiger' = esquire; possibly Slender uses the Italian form, more probably his Latinity is at fault; 1. 1. 8

AUTHENTIC, i.e. of established credit; 2. 2. 212

BAILLEZ, bring; 1. 4. 86

BANBURY CHEESE, a very thin cheese—referring to Slender's slenderness; Banbury was a notorious puritan centre and Bardolph may have this in mind also; 1. 1. 120

BARBASON, a prince of devils; cf. *Hen. V*, 2. 1. 57 and Scot, *Discoverie of Witchcraft*, xv. ii 'Marbas, alias Barbas, is a great president'; 2. 2. 274

BEAD, (*a*) a minute object; cf. *M.N.D.* 3. 2. 330; (*b*) prayer. N.B. It is Parson Hugh, albeit disguised, who gives him his holy commission; 5. 5. 49

BELL-WETHER, a ram with a bell at its neck to lead the flock. Ford led the 'rabble,' made much noise, and was a horned cuckold; 3. 5. 101

BETWEEN THIS AND HIS HEAD, a common phrase of the period in a similar connexion; 1. 4. 24

BILBO, a finely tempered sword, of Bilboa manufacture; 3. 5. 102

BOARD, (*a*) accost, address, (*b*) board a ship; 2. 1. 81–2

BOHEMIAN-TARTAR, v. *Hungarian*; 4. 5. 19

BOLD-BEATING, probably misprint for 'bowl-beating,' i.e. pot-thumping (v. note); 2. 2. 25

BOOK OF SONGS AND SONNETS, some miscellany of the period. Tottel's (1577) was entitled 'Songes and Sonettes'; 1. 1. 184

BOY (to her), a hunting cry (v.

Turbervile, *Booke of Hunting*, p. 114); 1. 3. 53

BRAINFORD, i.e. Brentford; 4. 2. 70, etc.

BREAD AND CHEESE, usually taken as referring to the frugal fare in Falstaff's service, but N.E.D. gives it as a name of the cuckoo-bread flower, which is the point required here. Falstaff is the cuckoo in Page's nest (cf. 'cuckoo-birds,' 2. 1. 113), and his bread is cuckoo-bread; 2. 1. 123

BRIBED-BUCK, stolen deer (v. note); 5. 5. 24

BUCK, (a) male deer, stag; (b) dirty linen to be steeped in alkaline lye, as the first process in buck-washing or bleaching (cf. *whitsters*); 3. 3. 150, etc.

BUCKLERSBURY, a London street for grocers and apothecaries, whose shops were full of herbs 'in simple-time'; 3. 3. 69

BULLY, i.e. gallant (a term of endearment); 1. 3. 3, etc. For 'bully-rook' v. note 1. 3. 3 and for 'bully-stale' v. *stale*

BURN DAY-LIGHT, i.e. waste time; 2. 1. 48

BUTTONS, ''tis in his buttons,' probably a misprint for 'talons' (v. note); 3. 2. 63

CABBAGE, i.e. cabbage-head = fool; note the transition to 'broke your head'; 1. 1. 114

CANARY, (a) a lively Spanish dance; (b) sweet wine from the Canaries (cf. *pipe-wine* and note 3. 2. 80); 3. 2. 79

CANARIES, Quickly's confusion between *canary* (a) and 'quandary'; 2. 2. 58

CANE-COLOURED, v. note; 1. 4. 21

CAREERS, 'passed the careers,' i.e. ran away with him (lit. 'galloped at full-speed over a race-course'), v. note; 1. 1. 166

CARRY, (i) 'carry-her,' probably Evans' pronunciation of 'career,' i.e. gallop; 1. 1. 222; (ii) 'carry't,' i.e. carry off the prize, v. note; 3. 2. 63

CARVE, make advances by signalling in a peculiar way with the fingers—'a sort of digitary ogle' (Lucas, *Webster* i. 209). Cf. *Err.* 2. 2. 121–2; *L.L.L.* 5. 2. 323 'A' can carve too and lisp' [1954], 1. 3. 44

CASHIER, (a) discard; (b) cheat, rob (? at cards); 1. 1. 165; 1. 3. 7

CASTILIAN-KING-URINAL, v. note; 2. 3. 30

CATAIAN, i.e. inhabitant of Cathay. The Elizabethans had news of the wiles of 'the heathen Chinee' before Bret Harte; 2. 1. 130

CAT-A-MOUNTAIN, wild cat; 2.2.24

CHARACTERY, symbolical writing; 5. 5. 73

CHARINESS, scrupulous integrity; 2. 1. 90

CHEATER, (a) escheator, an official of the Exchequer; (b) sharper; 1. 3. 68

CHEESE, the Welshman's love of cheese was a popular subject of jest at this period; 1. 2. 11; 2. 2. 280; 5. 5. 82, 135

CLAPPER-CLAW, maul, thrash; 2. 3. 60

CLERKLY, (a) like a scholar; (b) smartly, artfully (v. note); 4. 5. 53

COG, cheat (at dice-play); 3. 1. 114; 3. 3. 44, 67

COME OFF, pay up; 4. 3. 11

CONY-CATCH, swindle—a cant term; the cony (=rabbit) was the dupe; 1. 1. 117; 1. 3. 33

GLOSSARY

CORAM, i.e. quorum, a common corruption. Justices of Quorum, or Coram, were those who sat on the bench at county sessions; 1. 1. 5

CORNUTO, horned cuckold (v. *peaking*); 3. 5. 66

COSTARD, head (lit. a large apple); 3. 1. 14

COTSALL, i.e. the Cotswolds, a favourite resort for coursing-matches (spelt 'Cotsole,' 2 *Hen. IV*, 3. 2. 24; 'Cotshall,' *Ric. II*, 2. 3. 9); 1. 1. 84

COUNCIL, (a) Privy Council, Star-chamber (q.v.); (b) ecclesiastical synod; 1. 1. 31–3

COUNSEL (in), in private; 1. 1. 112

COUNTER-GATE, (a) gate of the debtor's prison, notorious for its smell (Falstaff had other reasons for his dislike); (b) ? = counter-gait, i.e. in the opposite direction; 3. 3. 75

COWL-STAFF, a stout pole passed through the handles of a 'cowl' (lit. a water-tub), so that it could be hoisted by two men; 3. 3. 139

COXCOMB, fool's cap, in reference to Evans' satyr-head; 5. 5. 134

CRIED-GAME, v. note; 2. 3. 81

CRY AIM, applaud (archery term); 3. 2. 40

CURTAL-DOG, a dog with a docked tail, of no service in the chase; 2. 1. 100

CUSTALORUM = contraction or corruption of 'custos rotulorum,' i.e. keeper of the rolls; 1. 1. 6

CUT AND LONG-TAIL, i.e. horses or dogs of all sorts. Slender means 'Let them all come—under the degree of a squire,' i.e. so long as they are not too grand; 3. 4. 46

DATCHET-MEAD, between Windsor Little Park and the Thames; 3. 3. 126, 141; 3. 5. 92

DAUBERY, false shows; 4. 2. 170

DECK (above), (a) above-board; (b) in reference to covering of any kind, clothes or sheets; 2. 1. 83

DEVIL-HERN, v. note; 5. 3. 11

DIFFUSÉD, generally interpreted 'disorderly,' but possibly 'dispersed' (cf. 'burthen dispersedly,' *Temp.* 1. 2. 384); 4. 4. 55

DISTANCE, v. *fencing*; 2. 1. 201; 2. 3. 23

DIVINITY, ? divination; 5. 1. 3

DRAFF, hog's wash; 4. 2. 100

DRUMBLE, loiter, be sluggish; 3. 3. 139

DUTCH DISH, the German fondness for greasy cooking was evidently known in Shakespeare's day. Dutch = German; 3. 5. 109

EDWARD SHOVEL-BOARDS, old broad shillings of Edward VI, worn smooth by age and use, and therefore convenient for the game of Shovel-board or Shove-groat (cf. 2 *Hen. IV*, 2. 4. 207) in which the coin was flipped along a polished board into holes at the end of it; v. *Sh. Eng.* ii. 467–8. Slender paid 2s. 3d. apiece, no doubt on account of their excellent smoothness! 1. 1. 145

EGRESS AND REGRESS, a legal phrase, meaning right of entry, especially into harbours and waterways; the Host is quibbling on the name 'Brook'; 2. 1. 194

ELD, antiquity; 4. 4. 36

ENTERTAIN, engage in battle; 1. 3. 53: treat; 2. 1. 78

EPHESIAN, boon companion (cf. 2 *Hen. IV*, 2. 2. 164 'Ephesians of the old church'); 4. 5. 16

EQUIPAGE, usually taken to mean camp-follower's pickings or

stolen goods; but 'in equipage' =step by step (v. N.E.D. 'equipage' 14), and Pistol probably means 'in instalments'; 2. 2. 1

ERINGOES, candied roots of seaholly, considered provocative; 5. 5. 20

ETHIOPIAN. The Host seems to have in mind 'Ethiops martial,' a metallic compound known to the old chemists and no doubt familiar to Dr Caius; 2. 3. 24

EVITATE, avoid; 5. 5. 219

EYAS-MUSKET, young male sparrowhawk; the musket was 'the smallest and most insignificant [of the breed], yet a very smart little hawk...If taken from the nest, as an eyas, it would be also one of the tamest and most docile' (*Sh. Eng.* ii. 363)—all which is most applicable to Robin; 3. 3. 20

FALL (v. note); 1. 1. 236

FALLOW, brownish-yellow; 1. 1. 83

FARTHINGALE (semi-circled), hooped skirt, extending behind but not in front of the body; 3. 3. 60

FAULT, (i) ''tis your fault.' This has puzzled many; but 'fault' = 'a check caused by failure of scent' and 'your' is used in a general sense (cf. 'your serpent in Egypt,' *Ant.* 2. 7. 29). The comment is quite in Shallow's usual manner (cf. ''tis the heart,' 2. 1. 202); 1. 1. 87. (ii) ''Tis my fault,' i.e. 'it is my misfortune'; 3. 3. 208

FEE'D, employed (lit. 'hired' like a servant, v. N.E.D.); 2. 2. 184

FEE-SIMPLE, WITH FINE AND RECOVERY (in), i.e. in absolute possession, under the strongest legal sanction (cf. *Sh. Eng.* i.

405–6). Mrs Page is perhaps thinking of the 'twenty pounds' (=fine) and the attempt to bring Falstaff to his senses in Act 5 (=recovery); 4. 2. 205–6

FELLOW OF THIS WALK, i.e. the keeper or forester of this beat, to whom would be due a shoulder after a kill. Windsor Forest was divided up into 'walks.' Falstaff quibbles, meaning that he will keep his shoulders to fight the keeper, should he appear; 5. 5. 25

FENCING (cf. 1. 1. 265–70; 2. 1. 198–204; 2. 3. 13–24), an innovation in Shakespeare's day. Justice Shallow, of the old school, sighs for the days of the long sword, which the new-fangled rapier has ousted. Dr Caius, as Frenchman, represents the new school (v. *Sh. Eng.* ii. 389–407). TERMS: *distance* = the regulation interval to be kept between the fencers; *foin, veney, stoccado* (or *stock*) and *punto* = different kinds of hits or thrusts; *reverse* = punto reverso or back-handed thrust; *montant* = the montanto or upright blow

FICO, Italian for 'fig'; 1. 3. 29

FIGHTS, canvas screens to conceal men on ship-board, before going into action; 2. 2. 128

FIGURE, (i) 'by the figure' = ?by astrological figures or by making waxen figures for the purpose of enchantment; 4. 2. 170. (ii) 'Scrape the figures' etc., i.e. clear your husband's brain of phantasms; 4. 2. 210

FIND YOU, unmask you: Evans seems to think he means to strip her; 4. 2. 135

FIXTURE, poise, tread; 3. 3. 58

FLANNEL, 'the Welsh flannel,' in

reference to Evans' disguise (v. note 5. 3. 11); flannel and frieze (q.v.) were of Welsh manufacture at this period; 5. 5. 158

FLAX, possibly misprint for 'flux,' i.e. a discharge of blood or other matter from the body (v. note); 5. 5. 147

FOIN, v. *fencing*; 2. 3. 21

FOPPERY, dupery, deceit; 5. 5. 120

FRAMPOLD, crusty, disagreeable; 2. 2. 86

FRANCISCO, Frenchman, with a quibble perhaps on 'francisc' = battle-axe; 2. 3. 25

FRETTED, worked, fermented (v. N.E.D. 'fret' vb. 10, which does not quote this passage). Cf. 'distillation'; Falstaff means that the clothes had enough grease of their own without his, to make them ferment; 3. 5. 104

FRIEZE, a coarse cloth with a nap, v. *flannel*; 5. 5. 134

FROTH AND LIME, 'to froth' = to give short measure by frothing the ale overmuch; 'to lime' = to mitigate the sourness of wine or ale by doctoring it with lime; 1. 3. 15

GALLIMAUFRY, medley, i.e. promiscuity; 2. 1. 105

GEMINY, pair; 2. 2. 9

GING, old form of 'gang'; 4. 2. 113

GOLIATH WITH A WEAVER'S BEAM, cf. 2 *Sam.* xxi. 19 'the staff of Goliath's spear was like a weaver's beam'; 5. 1. 20

GOOD AND FAIR (a technical expression), cf. Turbervile, *Booke of Hunting*, ch. 6 'the tokens whereby a man may knowe a good and fayre hound'; 1. 1. 91

GOOD EVEN AND TWENTY, i.e. good day and plenty of them! ('even' = any time after noon); 2. 1. 177

GOOD-JER (or 'good-year'), unexplained; N.E.D. describes it as 'a meaningless expletive,' but 'the good-years shall devour them flesh and fell' (*Lear* 5. 3. 24) implies something definite and evil; 1. 4. 119

GOT'S LORDS AND HIS LADIES, possibly Evans' expansion of the expletive 'God's lud' = God's Lord; 1. 1. 221

GOTTEN IN DRINK. Cowards were credited with this origin; 1. 3. 22

GOT-'UDGE ME, i.e. God judge me; 1. 1. 172

GOURD AND FULLAM, species of false dice; 1. 3. 84

GRATED, worried, pestered; 2. 2. 6

GREAT CHAMBER, large reception-room. These were a new feature in houses of this period and only found in those of the wealthy; Slender is bragging as usual (v. *Sh. Eng.* ii. 60); 1. 1. 144

GREEN-SLEEVES (the tune of), an amorous ballad-tune, associated somehow with harlotry: *Stat. Reg.* (Sept. 15, 1580) enters 'Greene Sleves moralised to the Scripture, declaringe the manifold benefites and blessinges of God bestowed on sinfull menne'; 2. 1. 57; 5. 5. 19

GROAT, 'seven groats in mill-sixpences'; a groat = fourpenny piece; mill-sixpences = newly introduced machine-made coins, with hard edges, to replace the older crudely hammered coins. 'Slender's words are *pour rire* in two senses, (*a*) the impossibility of reckoning the sum that way, (*b*) the confusion between the old groat (a time-honoured unit

of value with immemorial traditions) and the latest mechanical
improvement in coinage' (Prof.
George Unwin: privately); but
v. *British Numismatic Journ.*
3rd Ser. III, 291; I. I. 145

HACK, 'these knights will hack.'
'Hack' appears to mean 'to take
to the road as a highwayman,'
or (of a female) 'to become a
harlot' (cf. 'hackney,' *L.L.L.*
3. 1. 35). N.E.D. gives 'hack'
(vb.[3] 3*b*)='to ride on the road;
as distinguished from cross-
country or military riding,' but
quotes only 19th cent. instances.
Hart shows good reason for
thinking the jest refers to the
'Cales (i.e. Cadiz) Knights'
created by the Earl of Essex in
1596. Note the possibility of
word-play in 'Alice' and 'Cales'
or 'Calice'; this is the only
occasion on which we learn
Mrs Ford's Christian name;
2. 1. 46

HAPPY MAN BE HIS DOLE, pro-
verbial= may his dole (i.e. lot) be
that of a happy man; 3. 4. 65

HAVE WITH YOU, i.e. 'Let's go together'; 2. 1. 141, 197; 3. 2. 83

HAVING, property; 3. 2. 65

HAVIOUR, appearance; 1. 3. 77

HAWK FOR THE BUSH, a short-
winged hawk for quarry such as
pheasants, rabbits, etc. in wood-
land country (v. *Sh. Eng.* ii.
363–4); 3. 3. 221

HEART OF ELDER, i.e. of pith, as
contrasted with 'heart of oak';
2. 3. 26

HEROD OF JEWRY, a type of out-
rageous audacity (cf. *Ant.* 3. 3.
3); 2. 1. 17

HICK AND HACK, copulate. Cf.

Nashe, *Choice of Valentines,*
l. 114, and 'hackney' in G. of
L.L.L.; 4. 1. 59

HIGH AND LOW, false dice, so
loaded as to cast high or low
numbers at will; 1. 3. 85

HODGE-PUDDING, a large sausage of
boar's or hog's meat, still a dainty
in the West of England; 5. 5. 147

HOLE MADE IN YOUR BEST COAT,
proverbial= flaw in your reputation; 3. 5. 129

HONESTY, honour; 2. 1. 91, etc.

HORN-MAD, mad with rage like a
bull; 1. 4. 47; (with a quibble on
the cuckold's horn), 3. 5. 138

HOT= hit (v. note); 1. 1. 268

HOT BACKS, hot-backed= lustful;
5. 5. 11

HUNGARIAN, in [reference to discarded and cashiered soldiers
from Hungary (cf. 'base Phrygian
Turk' 1. 3. 87, 'Bohemian-Tartar' 4. 5. 19). In 1593 war broke
out between the Empire and the
Turks and lasted until 1606; 1.
3. 20

ILL, (*a*) savage, (*b*) miserable, which
is the meaning Mrs Ford takes
up (v. N.E.D.); 2. 1. 31

INSTALMENT, seat in which a
Knight of the Garter was in-
stalled; 5. 5. 63

INTOLERABLE, excessive; 5. 5. 149

JACK, knave; 1. 4. 55, 114

JACK-A-LENT, dressed-up puppet for
boys to throw at in Lent; 3. 3.
24; 5. 5. 122

JACK-AN-APES, lit. 'monkey,' but
Evans means a satyr, which was
a kind of 'ape' (v. note 5. 3. 11);
4. 4. 68

JAYS, symbolical of loose women; 3.
3. 39

GLOSSARY

KIBES, chilblains; 1. 3. 32

KISSING-COMFITS, perfumed sugar-plums, used by women to sweeten their breath; 5. 5. 20

KNOT, band, company; 3. 2. 46; 4. 2. 113

LABRAS, Pistol's blunder for 'labra,' lips; 1. 1. 152

LAROON, thief (v. note); 1. 4. 67

LATTEN, tin; 1. 1. 151

LEGEND OF ANGELS, i.e. legion of angels, but with a quibble on the Golden Legend (v. note); 1. 3. 52

LIFE IS A SHUTTLE. Cf. *Job* vii. 6 'My days are swifter than a weaver's shuttle'; 5. 1. 21

LIQUOR, grease, oil (vb.); 4. 5. 90

LUCE, (a) pike (fresh-water), (b) hake, cod (salt-water), v. *Introd.* pp. xxxv–xxxvii and note 1. 1. 20; 1. 1. 14, 19

LUNES, v. note; 4. 2. 20

LURCH, pilfer; 2. 2. 23

MARRY TRAP. N.E.D. does not explain, but Dr Johnson interprets 'an exclamation of insult, when a man was caught in his own stratagem' (cf. *Ham.* 3. 2. 247); 1. 1. 156

MECHANICAL SALT-BUTTER ROGUE, 'mechanical' = base, 'salt-butter' = (a) perhaps a contemptuous reference to Ford's station in life as a trader, (b) lecherous cuckold, 'butter' referring to the horn; 2. 2. 257

MELT ME OUT OF MY FAT. 'Fat' here has the secondary meaning of 'slow wit,' cf. 1 *Hen. IV*, 1. 2. 2 'fat-witted'; 4. 5. 89

MEPHOSTOPHILUS; 1. 1. 122. Pistol may be thinking of Marlowe's *Dr Faustus*, 1. 3. 32–3:

How pliant is this Mephostophilis:
Full of obedience and humility.

METHEGLINS, a Welsh variety of mead; 5. 5. 154

MIDDLE EARTH (man of), i.e. mortal (v. N.E.D. 'middle-erd'); 5. 5. 80

MILL-SIXPENCES, v. *groat*; 1. 1. 145

MINCE, i.e. trip it. Cf. *Isaiah* iii. 16 '...the daughters of Zion are haughty and walk with stretched forth necks and wanton eyes, walking and mincing as they go'; where the 1611 version explains 'mincing' as 'tripping nicely'; 5. 1. 8

MOCKED, (a) deceived, (b) ridiculed; 5. 3. 17–18

MOCK-WATER, v. note; 2. 3. 52

MONTANT, v. *fencing*; 2. 3. 24

MOUNTAIN-FOREIGNER, cf. 'mountain-squire' (*Hen. V*, 5. 1. 37); 1. 1. 150

MUMBUDGET. Cotgrave gives 'to play at Mumbudget, or be at a Non-plus,' and Nashe (McKerrow, iii. 124) uses it as the cry of one who is baffled; probably derived from some children's game. Surely Anne Page suggested this 'nay-word.' Note that Slender gets the 'budget'—of the postboy. 5. 2. 6; 5. 5. 190

MUMMY, a pulpy substance or mass (N.E.D.); 3. 5. 17

MUSSEL-SHELL, i.e. empty fool, perhaps with a quibble upon 'muzzle' (cf. note 4. 5. 50); 4. 5. 26

NAY-WORD, pass-word, watch-word; 2. 2. 118; 5. 2. 5

NO-VERBS, usually interpreted as 'words which do not exist,' but possibly = nay-words (q.v.); 3 1. 99

NURSE, housekeeper; 1. 2. 3; 3. 2. 58

NUTHOOK, i.e. catchpole, constable. 'Nutcrackers' was likewise a cant term for a pillory. N.B. the quibble in 'the very note of it'; 1. 1. 156

NYM, to nim = to steal, filch

OBSEQUIOUS, zealous, dutiful; 4. 2. 2

OD'S NOUNS, perversion of 'God's wounds'; 4. 1. 22

OEILLADES, sheep's eyes, amorous glances; 1. 3. 59

O'ER-LOOKED, i.e. with the evil eye; 5. 5. 83

OPEN, give tongue (like a hound); 4. 2. 192

OUPH, elf; lit. 'elf's child, change-ling'; 4. 4. 50; 5. 5. 57

OX, 'to make an ox of one' = to make one a fool; here with special reference to the horns (cf. *Troil.* 5. 1. 66); 5. 5. 116

OYES, i.e. 'oyez,' the crier's call; 5. 5. 41

PACK, plot, conspiracy; 4. 2. 113

PASSANT, (a) excellently, (b) heraldic term, 'of a beast, walking and looking towards the dexter side with one forepaw raised' (N.E.D.); 1. 1. 17

PEAKING CORNUTO, i.e. 'slinking (or prying) cuckold,' with a quibble upon 'peak,' i.e. the point of the horn; 3. 5. 66

PECK, a round vessel used as a peck measure; 3. 5. 102

PENSIONERS, i.e. 'the gentlemen pensioners' or royal body-guard. Quickly ranks them above earls on account of their splendid uniform (cf. *M.N.D.* 2. 1. 10); 2. 2. 73

PERIOD, goal; 3. 3. 42

PERPEND, ponder; 2. 1. 105

PHEAZAR, i.e. Vizier (Hart); 1. 3. 10

PHLEGMATIC, blunder for 'choleric'; Quickly attempts the talk of physicians; 1. 4. 74

PHRYGIAN TURK, v. *Hungarian*; 1. 3. 87

PICKT-HATCH, 'your manor of Pickthatch,' a disreputable quarter of London. Hart quotes Randolph, *Miser's Looking-glass*, 'my Pickthatch graunge and Shoreditch farm'; 2. 2. 17

PINK, v. note; 2. 2. 127

PINNACE, (a) a light vessel, often in attendance upon a larger one, (b) go-between, bawd. Hart quotes Heywood, *Edward IV*, pt i, 'Farewell, pink and pinnace, flibote and carvel'; 1. 3. 79

PIPE-WINE, v. note; 3. 2. 80

PITTIE-WARD, v. note; 3. 1. 5

PLUMMET, (a) a woollen fabric (N.E.D. 'plumbet')—quibble on 'flannel' (q.v.), (b) plummet-line, for fathoming; 5. 5. 158

POTATOES, i.e. the 'batata' or sweet potato, considered provocative; 5. 5. 19

POTTLE = 2 quarts; 2. 1. 191; 3. 5. 28

PRAT, prats = buttocks (N.E.D.). Ford is as good as his quibble; 4. 2. 178

PRECISIAN, puritan (v. note); 2. 1. 5

PREDOMINATE, an astrological term, carrying on the 'meteor' simile; 2. 2. 260

PREECHES, Evans means 'breeched,' i.e. whipped; 4. 1. 70

PREPARATIONS, accomplishments (N.E.D. gives no other instance of this meaning); 2. 2. 213

PRIMERO, a popular card-game (v. *Sh. Eng.* ii. 473); 4. 5. 93

GLOSSARY

PUDDINGS, sausages, entrails stuffed
with meat (cf. *hodge-pudding* and
1 *Hen. IV*, 2. 4. 498); 2. 1. 27
PUMPION, pumpkin; 3. 3. 38
PUNTO, v. *fencing*; 2. 3. 23

QUALITY, profession, business (cf.
Temp. 1. 2. 193); 5. 5. 40
QUEAN, hussy; 4. 2. 166
QUITTANCE, discharge from debt,
receipt; 1. 1. 9

RAG, worthless creature (N.E.D.);
4. 2. 179
RAGG'D, jagged; 4. 4. 31
RATOLORUM, Slender of course
means 'rotulorum' (v. *Custalorum*) and it seems possible that
Shakespeare intended him to say
so, the reading of the text being
a scribal error. The use of the
correct form would be sufficiently egregious here in itself,
since it shows that Slender is
unconscious that he is virtually
repeating Shallow's 'Custalorum'; 1. 1. 7
RATTLES, i.e. bladders with dried
peas or beans inside; 4. 4. 52
RAVENS (young), (*a*) cf. *Psal*. cxlvii.
9, (*b*) birds or beasts of prey
(N.E.D. 'ravin' 2 *b*, *c*), i.e.
sharks; 1. 3. 35
RED-LATTICE, i.e. of the ale-house—
red-lattice windows being commonly found in ale-houses; 2. 2. 25
REGISTER, catalogue; 2. 2. 175
RESPECT, reputation; 3. 1. 55
REVERSE, v. *fencing*; 2. 3. 23
RINGWOOD, popular Elizabethan
name for a hound (v. Golding's
Ovid, iii, 270); 2. 1. 108
RONYON, 'of obscure origin'
(N.E.D.), perhaps connected
with 'roinish,' 'ronyous' =
scabby (cf. *Macb*. 1.3.6); 4. 2. 180

SACK, general name for white Spanish or Canary wines; 2. 1. 8,
etc.; 'burnt sack,' i.e. hot drink
made of sack and sugar; 2. 1.
192, etc.
SACKERSON, a famous bear at Paris
garden in Shakespeare's day; 1.
1. 278
SADNESS, seriousness; 4. 2. 85
SALT-BUTTER, v. *mechanical salt-
butter*; 2. 2. 257
SAUCE THEM, i.e. make it hot for
them; 4. 3. 11
SCALL, i.e. 'scald,' scabby; 3. 1. 113
SCUT, (*a*) the short tail of a hare
or deer, (*b*) N.E.D. quotes 15th
cent. example = 'skirt,' which
may also be intended here; 5. 5.
18
SEA-COAL, i.e. coal brought by sea
from Newcastle, as distinguished
from charcoal; 1. 4. 8
SEASON, 'of the season,' i.e. in the
rutting-season; 3. 3. 152
SEESE, Welsh pronunciation of
'cheese' (q.v.); 1. 2. 11; 5. 5. 136
SENTENCES, 'out of his five sentences.' Possibly a blunder for
'senses' as Evans supposes; but
cf. Lyly, *Euphues* (Bond ii. 158),
'Hungry stomackes are not to
be fed with sayings against
surfettings, nor thirst to be
quenched with sentences against
drunkennesse,' which suggests
that Slender had a Book of
Moral Maxims in his library;
1. 1. 163
SHAFT OR BOLT ON'T (make a), proverbial = do one thing or another.
A shaft was an arrow for the
long-bow, a bolt a shorter one
for the cross-bow; if the wood
was too short for the one it
would do for the other (*Sh. Eng.*
ii. 381); 3. 4. 24

SHELVY, made of shelves or sand-banks; 3. 5. 14

SHENT, rated, scolded; 1. 4. 34

SHIP-TIRE, head-dress shaped like a ship, or having a ship-like ornament; 3. 3. 53

SHORT KNIFE AND A THRONG, i.e. the cut-purse's requisites; 2. 2. 16

SHOVEL-BOARDS, v. *Edward shovel-boards*; 1. 1. 145

SHOWER SING IN THE WIND (cf. *Temp.* 2. 2. 20). Possibly connected with the noise of missiles or arrows (note 'shoot point blank,' l. 31); 3. 2. 34

SIDES, i.e. thighs, loins; 5. 5. 25

SIMPLES, herbs. Dr Caius finds a Simple in his closet; 1. 4. 62

SIT AT, i.e. live at; 1. 3. 9

SLICE, generally taken as referring to the 'Banbury cheese'; but the three sharpers are challenging Slender to utter the 'matter in his head,' and 'slice' may therefore be the hawking term for 'mute'; cf. 'pass good humours' (1. 1. 155) and Wither, *Brit. Rememb.* (1628), 'Our Herneshaws, slicing backward, filth on those | Whose worths they dare not openly oppose,' which seems very apt to the present situation; 1. 1. 124

SLIGHTED, v. note; 3. 5. 9

SOFTLY-SPRIGHTED, a polite way of saying he was a coward; 1. 4. 22

SPRAG, mispronunciation of 'sprack' = brisk, alert; 4. 1. 74

STALE, (*a*) dupe, laughing-stock (v. N.E.D. 'stale' sb.³ 6), (*b*) urine of cattle, with a quibble upon 'bully' (i.e. bull), cf. 'Castilian-King-Urinal'; 2. 3. 26

STAND (a special), i.e. a sheltered position or covert for shooting at game (cf. *L.L.L.* 4. 1. 7–10; 3 *Hen. VI*, 3. 1. 1–4; *Sh. Eng.* ii. 386); 5. 5. 226

STAND, waste time with; 3. 3. 119

STAR-CHAMBER MATTER, the King's Council, sitting in the Star-chamber, exercised jurisdiction in regard to 'such offences as riots, slanders and libels, or even criticisms of magistrates.' In 1590 a deer-stealing case was before it (*Sh. Eng.* i. 384–5, ii. 162); 1. 1. 2

STARINGS, 'swearings and starings.' McKerrow (*Nashe*, iv. 100) writes: 'The two words are very frequently thus used in conjunction. To "stare" seems…to mean little more than to swagger, to behave in an overbearing and offensive manner'; 5. 5. 155; cf. 'stare,' 2. 2. 258

STEWED PRUNES, a common term for prostitutes from the 'stews' (v. note); 1. 1. 267

STILL SWINE EATS ALL THE DRAFF, proverb = 'the quiet sow eats all the hog's-wash or refuse'; 4. 2. 100

STOCCADOES, v. *fencing*; 2. 1. 201

STOCK = *stoccado*; 2. 3. 23

STONES, testicles; 1. 4. 109

STOPPED, stuffed; 3. 5. 103

STRAIN, disposition; 2. 1. 80; 3. 3. 176

SUBMISSION, confession; 4. 4. 11

SUCH ANOTHER NAN, cf. *Troil.* 1. 2. 282, 'You are such another woman,' where the meaning seems to be 'a very woman'; 1. 4. 145

SUFFERANCE, distress; 4. 2. 2

SURGE, i.e. of sweat; 3. 5. 111

SWINGE, (*a*) beat, (*b*) have sexual intercourse (v. N.E.D. 'swinge' vb. 1*e*); 5. 5. 179–80

TAKE, bewitch; 4. 4. 32

TALLOW, 'piss my tallow.' Cf. Turbervile, *Booke of Hunting* (1576), p. 45: 'During the time of their [i.e. the harts'] rut...their chief meat is the red mushroom or Todestoole which helpeth well to make them pysse their greace'; 5. 5. 14

TESTER, sixpence; 1. 3. 86

THRUMMED HAT, i.e. made of weaver's thrums, or possibly fringed with them so as to conceal the wearer's face; 4. 2. 72

TIGHTLY, safely, i.e. like a 'tight ship' (cf. *Temp.* 5. 1. 225); 1. 3. 78: soundly; 2. 3. 60

TINDERBOX, a hit at Bardolph's 'fiery exhalations'; 1. 3. 25

TIRE-VALIANT, some kind of fanciful head-dress; 3. 3. 53

TRIAL-FIRE, Hart quotes Fletcher, *Faithful Shepherdess*, 5. 2:
In this flame his finger thrust,
Which will burn him if he lust;
But if not away will turn
As loth unspotted flesh to burn;
5. 5. 84

TROW, wonder; 1. 4. 128; 2. 1. 57

TRUCKLE-BED, small couch on castors; 4. 5. 6

TURTLES, i.e. turtle-doves, proverbial for fidelity; 2. 1. 72; 3. 3. 39

U'NCOPE, unmuzzle (v. note and N.E.D. 'cope'); 3. 3. 157

UNKENNEL, unearth; kennel = fox's hole (cf. *Ham.* 3. 2. 86); 3. 3. 156

UNRAKED, i.e. not banked up with ashes to keep the fire in all night; 5. 5. 44

UNTAPIS, come out of cover or hiding, see OED; 3. 3. 158

URCHINS, hedgehogs, or devils in that form; 4. 4. 50

VAGRAM (cf. 'vagrom' *Ado*, 3.3.26), Evans gets confused between 'fragrant' (l. 19) and 'vagrant'; 3. 1. 24

VENEY, v. *fencing*; 1. 1. 267

VIZAMENTS, advisements. Evans means 'consider that seriously'; 1. 1. 35

VLOUTING-STOG, i.e. floutingstock = laughing-stock; 3. 1. 111; 4. 5. 74

WARRENER, rabbit-keeper, not a very fearsome antagonist, rabbits being gentle beasts; 1. 4. 25

WATCHED, i.e. caught in the act (cf. 2 *H. VI*, 1. 4. 45); 5. 5. 100

WEATHERCOCK, referring to the page's fantastic attire; a weathercock often had a pennon attached to it (cf. *L.L.L.* 4. 1. 96, 'What plume of feathers is he that indited this letter? What vane? What weathercock?'); 3. 2. 16

WHITING, bleaching; 3. 3. 125

WHITSTERS, bleachers; 3. 3. 13

WINK, close the eyes; 5. 5. 48

WITTOL, a contented cuckold; 2. 2. 274

YEA AND NO (by), a puritan expletive; 1. 1. 81; 1. 4. 92; 4. 2. 187

YELLOWS, i.e. jaundice, generally of horses, but being a disease of the liver, formerly supposed the seat of the passions, also used for jealousy in man (v. note); 1. 3. 98

YOKE, couple; 2. 1. 157

YOKES, v. note; 5. 5. 104

YOUTH IN A BASKET, proverbial = fortunate lover (Hart); 4. 2. 112